D0804084

FENG SHUI
DOS AND TABOOS
A GUIDE TO WHAT TO PLACE WHERE

Best Wishes!

ANGI MA WONG

PACIFIC HERITAGE BOOKS
PALOS VERDES

Feng Shui Dos and Taboos: A Guide to What to Place Where
Copyright © 2000 Angi Ma Wong ISBN 1-928753-01-9
1st printing 1999
2nd printing 2000
3rd printing 2002

All rights reserved. No part of this publication may be
reproduced, stored in a retrieval system or transmitted, in any
form, or by any means, electronic, mechanical, photocopying,
recording, or otherwise, without prior written permission of
Pacific Heritage Books.

For information, inquiries, orders, and author speaking
engagements, contact:
Pacific Heritage Books,
P.O. Box 3967, Palos Verdes,
California USA 90274-9547
(310) 541-8818phone (310) 541-7178 fax
www.wind-water.com
Author email: amawong@worldnet.att.net

Acknowledgements: My grateful appreciation and thanks go
to Master Yap Cheng Hai, my honored teacher.

Foreword from Grand Master Yap Cheng Hai

Feng Shui is a fascinating subject that has been part of my life for almost half a century. I have personally seen fortunes rise and fall due to the application or misapplication of feng shui. The correct advice has been known to improve one's health, improve relationships and bring about *life fulfillment*.

The study of feng shui is an intricate process, requiring patience and careful years of experience. Simple improvements require obvious placements and changes to be made. However, intricate formulas, measuring positional, locations and time dimensional energies that can change lives are the subjects that fascinate and confound people worldwide.

Hectic work schedules and limited time mean many people simply do not have the patience to study and research the Art. Some find complicating applications of Feng Shui too overwhelming and perhaps too arduous. What the general public craves is a simplified version with simple methods. Methods that they can implement immediately without too much hassle.

One good feng shui tip is a precious jewel. One good applicable tip is worth its weight in gold. This book is a virtual goldmine of nuggets that can be applied to make simple and effective changes in your lives!

I had the good fortune of having Angi Wong attend my class in Los Angeles. A talented, knowledgeable and humble person, Angi proved her potential again in this book. I was honored to receive an invitation for a foreword and to see a student doing so well.

I congratulate her on her excellent book. I hope it will prove a stepping stone to many readers out there. May it bring you as much success, fun and good fortune as feng shui has brought me.

Yap Cheng Hai, Co-Founder
Yap Cheng Hai Feng Shui Center of Excellence
http://www.ychfengshui.com

Other titles by Angi Ma Wong:

☯ **Feng Shui Room-by-Room Home Design Kit** (March 2002)
❖ **Feng Shui Dos and Taboos for Love** (September 2002)
☯ **Feng Shui Dos and Taboos Page a Day Calendar**
   for 2003, 2004, 2005
❖ **Feng Shui Dos and Taboos for Financial Success** (2003)
☯ **Feng Shui Desk for Success Tool Kit**
❖ **Feng Shui Garden Design Kit**
☯ **Designing Your Garden with Feng Shui**
❖ **Feng Shui Wheel**
☯ **The Wind/Water Wheel:**
   A Feng Shui Tool for Transforming Your Life
❖ **Chinese Lunar New Year Song** (Bilingual CD)
☯ **Woman's 4-Minute Bible:**
   Lifelong Lessons for Personal Empowerment
❖ **Baby Boomer's 4-Minute Bible:**
   Enduring Values to Live By
☯ **Been There, Done That:**
   16 Secrets for Success for Entrepreneurs
❖ **Night of the Red Moon**
☯ **TARGET: The U.S. Asian Market**
   A Practical Guide to Doing Business

A Personal Message from Angi Ma Wong

I returned from speaking at the London International Feng Shui Conference motivated and inspired, so much that the idea for this book was born. Thanks to so many of you, audiences and readers alike, for your enthusiasm for this book and contributing to its remarkable success by word of mouth. Your calls and email telling me it's the best feng shui book you've read is most appreciated! Only 8 months old, and we're into another printing.

Keep in mind, that whatever you place where, do everything with a pure heart, strong intent, and in moderation. You *can* overdo a good thing. Strive, above all, for harmony and balance, in your life and in your environment. Feng shui needs to be practiced in concert with your spiritual, emotional and physical health. Practicing this ancient art of placement while neglecting these other aspects of your life weakens its effectiveness. Remember too, the other components of your destiny: fate, luck, charity, philanthropy, and education and self-development.

Pay attention to and keep a journal of the feng shui changes you have made, note and record when and what happens after you implement them. Be patient, for as I like saying, there is a reason and season for everything in our lives. Sometimes your results come quickly, while others take longer, depending on the strength of your faith and intentions, and remember that feng shui is as much about symbolism as it is about placement.

About a decade ago, the few of us practitioners all knew of and respected each other's work. Since then, feng shui has captured the imagination of the media and is now trendy. There are many schools of feng shui, some that have been around less than twenty years. Anyone who has taken a class or read a few books can have cards printed, claim to be an "expert," consult others, or even write a book. All add to the awareness, acceptance, and the confusion about feng shui, so choose your teacher, consultant, and books wisely. Remember that wisdom and knowledge comes as much if not more from experience than from book learning.

My personal spin about feng shui's global appeal and popularity is that it coincides with the spiritual black hole in so many people's lives. In the past millennium, humankind's focus and achievements have mostly centered around medicine, science, and technology. But for all the gadgets, inventions, and equipment we surround ourselves with and use, it is a paradox that we are working longer and harder than any other generation before us. We spend so much of our time in front of and in machines, that a great deal of our humanity has been lost.

Feng shui offers a return to a simpler, more intuitive, natural way of living that fulfills a deep need in impoverished spirits. It has been a vital and integral part of my Chinese upbringing, personal and professional life. I love sharing it with all of you to help you achieve the serenity as well as peace of mind and heart that I enjoy.

When you drink the water, remember its source. -*Chinese proverb*

Feng shui origins are in China and I thank those of you who share my mission and passion to keep feng shui close to its Chinese roots. By practicing traditional, classical Compass School feng shui, integrated with Form School, Eight Mansions, Flying Star and Four Pillars and other traditional forms throughout my consulting practice for many years, I feel that I share Grand Master Yap's vision of excellence.

May my endeavors guide and ease your journey to recapture your soul, and may good *chi* follow so that you may rediscover and reclaim your own personal power.

It is my gift to you for the new millennium.

Angi Ma Wong
Feng Shui Lady ™

TABLE OF CONTENTS

I Feng Shui Basics
II. What to Place Where

TABLE OF CONTENTS

TABLE OF CONTENTS

TABLE OF CONTENTS

**Dedicated to all teachers,
especially mine**
and
in memory of Daddy
Shiu-Tong Ma
who modeled a love of
learning, reading and writing and
contributed so much to this book
and its remarkable success

Teachers open the door...you enter yourself.
-Chinese proverb

**Everyone in the world knows more
about something than you.
Be humble and learn from each of them.**
-Angi Ma Wong

I

FENG SHUI BASICS

Throughout civilization, humankind has recognized the power and beauty of nature and the universe. All over the world, cultures have believed that spirits dwelled around them in nature, the weather, the flora and fauna-things they could not explain, but intuitively sensed possessed something different and special. Even primitive peoples acknowledged and identified certain places in their surroundings that they recognized as being unique to their senses: a rock, grove, tree, mountain, river, cave, or other natural places that they regarded to be sacred and holy.

To the ancient Chinese, that feeling was captured in the philosophy of feng shui, literally, "wind-water." Believing that their departed ancestors were forever connected in spirit with them, families sought to honor them by selecting their optimum final resting places. Male children were desired not only to carry on the family name, but because only they were permitted to clean the graves of departed family members. Even today, many Chinese still associate the practice of feng shui with death and dying.

This Chinese environmental art of placement is one of the five components of a person's destiny. First is fate, determined by heaven and over which you have no control or say. It is that which dictates who, when, how, why, and what you are at the moment of your birth. Luck follows after you are born, in the form of pure luck, man-made luck, and heaven luck. Thirdly, is feng shui, or earth luck. Fourth are charity and philanthropy and finally, education, experience, and self development.

I like using the analogy that life is much like a journey from one place to another. You may start out in a particular circumstance, but the choices and decisions you make determine in which mode of transportation you travel during your trip. The latter three components are the proactive things you can do to make changes along your journey.

The three major concepts of feng shui are the flow of energy, the balance of *yin* and *yang*, and the interaction of the five elements. You will also recognize these to be the foundation of traditional Chinese medicine (TCM), *tai chi, chi gong*, acupuncture, acupressure, herbal cures, and other Chinese medical practices.

In nature, we only find perfectly straight lines in very short segments, as in the canes of sugar and bamboo. Even the tallest redwoods and pines have irregularities, and it is a natural law that energy flows in wavy lines like the breezes, mountains, and streams. When they travel in straight paths, such as a roaring flood, its awesome power is unleashed.

When we see a river destroying everything in its path through the center of a town, we notice that the water is usually following something man-made such as a road. Freeways, tunnels, bridges, buildings, corners of buildings, lamp posts, etc. all have straight edges which are considered conduits of negative energy called *sha ch'i* or "killing energy." Therefore in feng shui, straight lines, the angles and corners they create "poison and killing arrows."

The duality of the universe and the world around us is expressed in the *tai chi*, a circle created by a light and a dark droplet, positioned end to end. *Yin* is female, soft, passive, nurturing, dark, fluid, even numbers and the right side of our bodies. *Yang* is male, bright, hard, active, aggressive, odd numbers and the left side of our bodies. The two comprise a whole, and yet there is an element of each in the other.

Dividing the two halves is a fluid S line which moves, according to the balance in the universe, nature, the environment surrounding us, and in us. Sometimes we have too much *yang*, and other times, we have too much *yin*. It is up to us to personally find and maintain the balance between the two in our physical, mental, emotional, spiritual, sexual, and intellectual selves. Achieving this balance is being grounded or centered...much like a rock that is pounded by the elements and still remains unyielding.

Then at last, are the five elements: fire, earth, metal, water, and wood. Each one of them relates to the other in two different ways. The first is in a generative or creative manner that gives strength and power to all. The second relationship is one that shows how each can be overcome or destroyed. Knowing the two cycles is critical in feng shui and placement for misinformation or lack of knowledge can bring on the opposite effect of what you are trying to achieve.

Relationships of the Elements

(diagram generative/destructive)

GENERATIVE Cycle

(Circle) Fire generates earth
Earth generates metal
Metal generates water
Water generates wood
Wood generates fire

DESTRUCTIVE Cycle

(Star) Fire melts metal
Metal cuts wood
Wood moves earth
Earth dams water
Water puts out fire

Two of the most popular forms of feng shui are the Compass School and the Black (Hat) Sect Tantric Tibetan Buddhist School. Others include Flying Star, Taoist, Four Pillars, Form, and Intuitive. For thousands of years, Compass School has been recognized as the traditional, classical feng shui practice which uses either a Chinese (*luo pan*) or Western-style compass to determine the exact direction of the main entrance to your rooms, office or home.

Because the eight compass directions govern various aspects of your life, you would then place the corresponding colors, animal symbols, numbers, and elements in those areas that you want to activate. In the BSTB school, popularized in the past 20-something years, you would totally disregard compass directions, stand at and use the *entrance* of the room, house, or office as your main reference point. Then using that point always as Career, you would place objects and other enhancements according to the different *aspirations and accomplishments* of your life that you want to activate or achieve. (For details, see **BAGUA**)

Whichever form of feng shui you choose to practice, be consistent and practical. If you do not get the results that you seek, feel free to try others. The guidelines remain basically the same: put the right objects in the right place to be in harmony and balance with yourself, nature, and the universe. Meanwhile, you will also be activating the various areas of your life that you wish to improve: harmony, health, love, romance, marriage, children, business, career, creativity, self-development, wealth, fortune, fame, and aspirations.

I have created the acronym CANE: **C** for color; **A** for animal symbol; **N** for Number; **E** for Element to help you remember what to put in each area according to general feng shui. Basically, you put the C, A, N and E of each direction in that direction if you want to improve/attract that aspect of your life. You can also add the element that *precedes* it in the generative cycle to strengthen your efforts. On the other hand, to suppress an element, introduce its 'destroyer" or the one that follows it in the destructive cycle to exhaust or weaken it.

In addition to placement, you need to be mindful that everything in the world and universe is constantly changing. Each year, what is known as the **3 Afflictions** exert yearly influences that supersede your feng shui. Pay particular attention to where these areas are located annually, and take the following special precautions beginning on the first day of the Chinese new year (see p. 23.) Your efforts will be well rewarded to avert major mishaps, ill health, and misfortune to you and your family, at home and work.

The direction of the first Affliction, **Grand Duke Jupiter,** cannot be disturbed in any way. **Do not** sit facing this direction, but you may sit with your back toward it, so that he can provide support to you.

Don't dig, demolish, construct, plant, install, or in any way disturb the ground in this direction during the year. **Do** put the corresponding element or Chinese zodiac animal symbol (see p. 23) in the direction he is located to control him, which affects 15°.

The **3 Killings,** based on the Chinese zodiac animals and like the Grand Duke, cannot be disturbed in any way with construction, digging, demolition, cutting, pruning, etc. It always occurs in one of the cardinal directions: N,S, E, W. *Unlike* the Grand Duke, you can *sit in* or *face* the 3 Killings during the year, affecting the 45° which includes this direction. Mishaps and bad luck will occur in the zodiac years in which the animals are deemed incompatible and unfortunate matches. This always occurs when the partners are six years apart in age.

☆ My husband is six years older than I, he being born in the Year of the Snake, and I in that of the Boar. When his zodiac animal year comes up, I should take extra precautions and lay low, and during the Year of the Boar, he should do the same.

LOCATIONS OF THE THREE AFFLICTIONS 1999-2012				
Year begins	Zodiac Animal	Grand Duke Jupiter in	3 Killings is in	5 Yellows is in
2/16/99	Rabbit	E	W	S
2/5/00	Dragon	E/SE	S	N
1/24/01	Snake	S/SE	E	SW
2/12/02	Horse	S	N	E
2/1/03	Ram	S/SW	W	SE
1/22/04	Monkey	W/SW	S	Center
2/9/05	Rooster	W	E	NW
1/29/06	Dog	W/NW	N	W
2/18/07	Boar	N/NW	W	NE
2/7/08	Rat	N	S	S
1/26/09	Ox	N/NE	E	N
2/14/10	Tiger	E/NE	N	SW
2/3/11	Rabbit	E	W	E
1/23/12	Dragon	E/SE	S	SE

Grand Duke Jupiter (affects 15 degrees): It is okay to have this direction <u>behind</u> you, but do not face this way. **3 Killings** (affects 45 degrees and the opposite "shadow" direction across the compass): It is okay to face this direction, but do not have this direction <u>behind</u> you. Use a dragon tortoise sitting on a copy of the Lo Shu Square to suppress this Affliction. **5 Yellows** (affects 90 degrees): Most dangerous of all, do not touch/change anything in this direction all year. If you have a door that faces this direction and there is a close mountain or hill there, try not use it if possible. To do so is to invite illness, misfortune, calamity, and disaster to yourself and your family. Use a brass pagoda windchime to suppress it. **Regarding <u>all</u> of the Afflictions:** It is imperative <u>not to</u> disturb, construct, demolish, dig in these directions during the *entire* lunar year!

Do use a <u>dragon</u> tortoise or *chi ling* <u>to suppress the ill</u> <u>effects of the 3 Killings</u>. If it occurs in the direction of your front entrance, keep a bright light on there.

In the Years of the Monkey, Rat, and Dragon, the 3 Killings occur in the South (fire), so you should use the element of water to destroy it. In the Years of the Horse, Dog, and Tiger, it occurs in the North (water), so you would use the element of earth to suppress it. In the Years of the Rabbit, Sheep, and Boar, the 3 Killings is located in West (metal), so use the fire element to destroy it. Lastly, in the Years of the Snake, Rooster, and Ox, this Affliction occurs in the East (wood), so metal is the element you use to mitigate its effects.

The most powerful and dangerous of all yearly influences goes by the name of the **5 Yellows**. **Do not** <u>touch, move, dig,</u> <u>construct, build, prune</u> – in general, <u>disturb *anything* in the entire</u> <u>90° range of this compass direction during the year</u>. To do so is to bring about major disaster and calamity to you, your family, and your life.

☆ I know now that in 1989 when I began the major remodeling and addition to my home, I violated the SE/S realm of the 5 Yellows on my property and home, resulting in the most unforgettably disastrous time of my life, including the discovery of cancer and other major troubles. Moreover, 1989 was the Year of the Snake, which as mentioned earlier, was also particularly inauspicious for me. My daughter was hospitalized within a week of my activating a pump in the pond located in the North in May of 2000. Even Master Yap tells of how his entire family fell ill when he moved the earth one year in the direction of the 5 Yellows.

☆ My Newport Beach client Satinder fell ill within days after earth moving equipment arrived and started excavating on the hill located in South across the street from her home.

✮ But the most dramatic example of the the 5 Yellows' awesome power is that of the multi-million-dollar Ocean Trails Golf Course on California's Palos Verdes peninsula. Over a decade in planning before the work began, on June 2, 1999, a month before opening day, eleven acres of the cliffside course slid into the Pacific Ocean, taking the 18th hole along with it. I took a compass reading at the location of the slide and where the excavating and grading had been. Sure enough, the massive land movement had occurred in the South-facing coastline, where the 5 Yellows was at that year.

In 1999, the Grand Duke was located in the East, the 3 Killings in the West, and the 5 Yellows in the South. You could have changed your desk chair to face West so as not to confront the Grand Duke. In all three directions, you would not disturb the earth. Having experienced great misfortune ten years before, the remodeling at my home in 1999 took place in the unaffected areas of North, Northwest, and Northeast.

Last, but not least, **personalize** your feng shui by discovering your four best (and worst) directions based on your horoscope, for the day, month and year in which you were born each carry its own energy. In feng shui, you should FACE your best directions in order to RECEIVE the benefits of each coming to you. **Appendix A** gives easy-to-use instructions on how to do this.

✮ ✮ ✮

Much, if not most, of what you will do is based on good common sense, sound architectural design, intuition, geography, ecology, meteorology, astronomy, interior design, ancient Chinese philosophies such as Taoism, Buddhism, and folk beliefs that have survived thousands of years. These are the keys to creating good feng shui as you tap into the *tao*, or path or flow of the universe and its rhythms for a more holistic, natural and simple way of life.

Keep your heart pure and your intent strong and see how this fascinating and wonderful tradition transforms your life.

II

WHAT TO PLACE WHERE

ALTARS

These are important spots in your home or business and it is imperative that they be <u>located in an undisturbed place of honor, and respect</u>. Traditionally, altars in temples and monasteries are facing toward the west where it is believed that all Chinese gods dwell, but you can <u>place your altar in your 4th best direction</u>.

Do

❖ Put your altar in a quiet location away from the traffic flow.

❖ Keep your altar covered or indoors under some sort of shelter.

❖ Locate it across from your front door or in the NW which represents heaven and father, the head of the household.

❖ Put any statues of deities up in a high spot, above the height of the tallest person.

❖ If the bedroom is the only place for your altar, locate it away from or past the end of the bed and not on a shelf above the bed.

❖ Clean and maintain your altar.

❖ Throw away dried flowers, fruit, incense, and other offerings that are past their prime.

❖ Light your altar with artificial lighting or candles.

Don't

᷾ Put your altar in an area near, around, next to, sharing a wall with, under or across from any toilets, bathrooms, stairs or staircases.

᷾ Put your altar under any beams or in a bedroom where there is regular sexual activity as this is considered very unlucky.

ANIMALS

Animals have their own energy and symbolize different things. The twelve animals honored in the Chinese zodiac are used to determine one's personality as well as project compatibility between the signs.

There are two versions of the story about how these particular twelve animals of all in the world were honored with a year named after them. In the first, Buddha was lying on his deathbed and summoned all the living creatures of the world to visit him before he died. Only twelve made the effort and the great teacher named a year after each of them.

In the second story, the Jade Emperor announced the great race to determine the swiftest animals in the universe. They all lined up and made a dash as soon as the Emperor lowered his sepulcher. Wily Rat told Cat that the Great Race was on another day and when it was all over, the feline had missed the entire event. To this day, Cat still chases the Rat for tricking him!

During the race itself, the Rat hitched a ride on the back of the Ox who was leading. As it approached the finish, Rat jumped off and scurried across the line to win the race.

Remember that you cannot rely upon the information on the place mat that you saved from a Chinese restaurant. One day off, and you were born in an entirely different animal year with a very different personality and destiny!

The chart on the next page gives the exact dates of the beginning of all Chinese new years from 1900 to 2018 with the corresponding *kua* numbers for both men and women. You will use the *kua* number as a means to determining your best four and worst directions found in Appendix A.

Chinese Lunar New Year and Zodiac Animal Chart
(1900 - 2018)
Excerpted from **Wind-Water Wheel** © Angi Ma Wong 1996

inning Date	Ending Date	Animal Year	(M)en's Kua#	(W)omen's Kua#	Beginning Date	Ending Date	Animal Year	(M)en's Kua#	(W)omen's Kua#
/31/1900	2/18/01	Rodent	1M	5W	1/28/60	2/14/61	Rodent	4M	2W
/19/01	2/7/02	Ox	9M	6W	2/15/61	2/4/62	Ox	3M	3W
/8/02	1/28/03	Tiger	8M	7W	2/5/62	1/24/63	Tiger	2M	4W
/29/03	2/15/04	Rabbit	7M	8W	1/25/63	2/12/64	Rabbit	1M	5W
/16/04	2/3/05	Dragon	6M	9W	2/13/64	2/1/65	Dragon	9M	6W
/4/05	1/24/06	Snake	5M	1W	2/2/65	1/20/66	Snake	8M	7W
/25/06	2/12/07	Horse	4M	2W	1/21/66	2/8/67	Horse	7M	8W
/13/07	2/1/08	Ram	3M	3W	2/9/67	1/29/68	Ram	6M	9W
/2/08	1/21/09	Monkey	2M	4W	1/30/68	2/16/69	Monkey	5M	1W
/22/09	2/9/10	Rooster	1M	5W	2/17/69	2/5/70	Rooster	4M	2W
/10/10	1/29/11	Dog	9M	6W	2/6/70	1/26/71	Dog	3M	3W
/30/11	2/17/12	Boar	8M	7W	1/27/71	1/14/72	Boar	2M	4W
/18/12	2/5/13	Rodent	7M	8W	1/15/72	2/2/73	Rodent	1M	5W
/6/13	1/25/14	Ox	6M	9W	2/3/73	1/22/74	Ox	9M	6W
/26/14	2/13/15	Tiger	5M	1W	1/23/74	2/10/75	Tiger	8M	7W
/14/15	2/2/16	Rabbit	4M	2W	2/11/75	1/30/76	Rabbit	7M	8W
/3/16	1/22/17	Dragon	3M	3W	1/31/76	2/17/77	Dragon	6M	9W
/23/17	2/10/18	Snake	2M	4W	2/18/77	2/6/78	Snake	5M	1W
/11/18	1/31/19	Horse	1M	5W	2/7/78	1/27/79	Horse	4M	2W
/1/19	2/19/20	Ram	9M	6W	1/28/79	2/15/80	Ram	3M	3W
/20/20	2/7/21	Monkey	8M	7W	2/16/80	2/4/81	Monkey	2M	4W
/8/21	1/27/22	Rooster	7M	8W	2/5/81	1/24/82	Rooster	1M	5W
/28/22	2/15/23	Dog	6M	9W	1/25/82	2/12/83	Dog	9M	6W
/16/23	2/4/24	Boar	5M	1W	2/13/83	2/1/84	Boar	8M	7W
/5/24	1/24/25	Rodent	4M	2W	2/2/84	2/19/85	Rodent	7M	8W
/25/25	2/12/26	Ox	3M	3W	2/20/85	2/8/86	Ox	6M	9W
/13/26	2/1/27	Tiger	2M	4W	2/9/86	1/28/87	Tiger	5M	1W
/2/27	1/22/28	Rabbit	1M	5W	1/29/87	2/16/88	Rabbit	4M	2W
/23/28	2/9/29	Dragon	9M	6W	2/17/88	2/4/89	Dragon	3M	3W
/10/29	1/29/30	Snake	8M	7W	2/5/89	1/26/90	Snake	2M	4W
/30/30	2/16/31	Horse	7M	8W	1/27/90	2/14/91	Horse	1M	5W
/17/31	2/5/32	Ram	6M	9W	2/15/91	2/3/92	Ram	9M	6W
/6/32	1/25/33	Monkey	5M	1W	2/4/92	1/22/93	Monkey	8M	7W
/26/33	2/13/34	Rooster	4M	2W	1/23/93	2/9/94	Rooster	7M	8W
/14/34	2/3/35	Dog	3M	3W	2/10/94	1/30/95	Dog	6M	9W
/4/35	1/23/36	Boar	2M	4W	1/31/95	2/18/96	Boar	5M	1W
/24/36	2/10/37	Rodent	1M	5W	2/19/96	2/6/97	Rodent	4M	2W
/11/37	1/30/38	Ox	9M	6W	2/7/97	1/27/98	Ox	3M	3W
/31/38	2/18/39	Tiger	8M	7W	1/28/98	2/15/99	Tiger	2M	4W
/19/39	2/7/40	Rabbit	7M	8W	2/16/99	2/4/2000	Rabbit	1M	5W
/8/40	1/26/41	Dragon	6M	9W	2/5/00	1/23/01	Dragon	9M	6W
/27/41	2/14/42	Snake	5M	1W	1/24/01	2/11/02	Snake	8M	7W
/15/42	2/4/43	Horse	4M	2W	2/12/02	1/31/03	Horse	7M	8W
/5/43	1/24/44	Ram	3M	3W	2/1/03	1/21/04	Ram	6M	9W
/25/44	2/12/45	Monkey	2M	4W	1/22/04	2/8/05	Monkey	5M	1W
/13/45	2/1/46	Rooster	1M	5W	2/9/05	1/28/06	Rooster	4M	2W
/2/46	1/21/47	Dog	9M	6W	1/29/06	2/17/07	Dog	3M	3W
/22/47	2/9/48	Boar	8M	7W	2/18/07	2/6/08	Boar	2M	4W
/10/48	1/28/49	Rodent	7M	8W	2/7/08	1/25/09	Rodent	1M	5W
/29/49	2/16/50	Ox	6M	9W	1/26/09	2/13/10	Ox	9M	6W
/17/50	2/5/51	Tiger	5M	1W	2/14/10	2/2/11	Tiger	8M	7W
/6/51	1/26/52	Rabbit	4M	2W	2/3/11	1/22/12	Rabbit	7M	8W
/27/52	2/13/53	Dragon	3M	3W	1/23/12	2/9/13	Dragon	6M	9W
/14/53	2/2/54	Snake	2M	4W	2/10/13	1/30/14	Snake	5M	1W
/3/54	1/23/55	Horse	1M	5W	1/31/14	2/18/15	Horse	4M	2W
/24/55	2/11/56	Ram	9M	6W	2/19/15	2/7/16	Ram	3M	3W
/12/56	1/30/57	Monkey	8M	7W	2/8/16	1/27/17	Monkey	2M	4W
/31/57	2/17/58	Rooster	7M	8W	1/28/17	2/15/18	Rooster	1M	5W
/18/58	2/7/59	Dog	6M	9W	2/16/18	2/4/19	Dog	9M	6W
/8/59	1/27/60	Boar	5M	1W					

Here is the list of the animals in order with their corresponding directions, element, time of day and the exact locations on the compass each governs. It is believed that the 30 degrees in your house that matches your animal sign is very auspicious for you and that your hour is lucky for you.

Rat: North, water, 11p.m.-1 a.m., 337.5 to 7.5°
    Compatible with: Dragon, Monkey, Ox
    Incompatible with: Horse
Ox: North/Northeast, earth, 1-3 a.m., 7.5 to 37.5°
    Compatible with: Snake, Rooster, Rat
    Incompatible with: Horse, Dog, Ram
Tiger: East/Northeast, wood, 3-5 a.m., 37.5 to 67.5°
    Compatible with: Horse, Dragon, Dog
    Incompatible with: Snake, Monkey
Hare: East, wood, 5-7 a.m., 67.5 to 97.5°
    Compatible with: Ram, Boar, Dog
    Incompatible with: Rooster, Rat
Dragon: East/Southeast, earth, 7-9 a.m., 97.5 to 127.5°
    Compatible with: Rat, Snake, Monkey
    Incompatible with: Ox, Hare, Dragon
Snake: South/Southeast, fire, 9-11 a.m., 127.5 to 157.5°
    Compatible with: Ox, Rooster
    Incompatible with: Ram, Dog, Tiger
Horse: South, fire, 11 a.m. – 1 p.m., 157.5 to 187.5°
    Compatible with: Tiger, Dog, Ram
    Incompatible with: Ox, Hare, Horse
Ram: South/Southwest, earth, 1-3 p.m., 187.5 to 217.5°
    Compatible with: Hare, Boar, Horse
    Incompatible with: Rat, Ox, Dog
Monkey: West/Southwest, metal, 3-5 p.m., 217.5 to 247.5°
    Compatible with: Dragon, Rat
    Incompatible with: Tiger, Snake, Boar
Rooster: West, metal, 5-7 p.m., 247.5 degrees to 277.5°
    Compatible with: Ox, Snake, Dragon
    Incompatible with: Rat, Rooster, Dog

Dog: West/Northwest, earth, 7-9 p.m., earth, 277.5 to 307.5°
  Compatible with: Horse, Tiger, Hare
  Incompatible with: Rooster, Dragon
Boar. North/Northwest, water, 9-11 p.m., 307.5 to 337°
  Compatible with: Rat, Ox, Dragon
  Incompatible with: Monkey, Boar, Snake

The twelve animals of the Chinese Zodiac give information about personalities and are used for matchmaking as well predicting one's luck and fortune. When the dozen images are combined in art and or worn in jewelry or on clothing, they represent protection and good luck. You can also wear or use images of the specific animal that corresponds to your birth year.

The five noxious animals in Chinese culture are the gecko, centipede, snake, scorpion, and the toad. Especially dangerous is the centipede whose many legs resemble a human spine with many sections, and portends grave misfortune and illness (see **Rooster**.)

Do
❖ Wear and decorate with the Chinese zodiac animal which corresponds to your birth year or the set of all twelve animals together.

❖ Keep a bird or fish for a pet as both represent wealth.

❖ Your pet bird should ideally be uncaged because to keep it confined means that your wealth will be limited.

❖ Keep a red bird like a parrot for protection, and in the S.

❖ The pet should match the color of the season in which you were born. For example, if you were born in summer, keep a red bird or fish; green for spring; white for autumn; black for winter.

Do

❖ If you keep fish in your office, their color should match that of your *wife*'s birth season.

❖ Hang any bird feathers you find around or near your front door. They represent protection to you and your family.

❖ Give bird feathers as a thoughtful gift to family and friends.

❖ If your feathers blow away, try to find others to replace them.

Don't

☞ Ask for feathers from others.

☞ Throw feathers away, but rather keep them for protection.

Here are some other animal symbols used in feng shui:

Unlike in Western culture, **bats** are common in Chinese motives to represent happiness, good fortune, long life, and protection. Use in SW for marital happiness.

Cow/Ox (also bull, etc.) is a revered animal that is the second animal in the cycle of the zodiac, representing spring. It is honored because it pulls the plow to prepare the fields from which harvest and sustenance come. The cow represents the female, and in Buddhism, eating beef is banned.

A wish-fulfilling cow is really an ox reclining on a mound of coins and ingots, sometimes with a figure on its back. **Do** put a wooden figurine on your desk, in SE or E for wealth; those of metal in W or NW; ceramic ones in SW or NE.

A **deer** represents long life, speed, prosperity, endurance, wealth, and riches. **Do** display figurines of this animal in the compass direction that matches its element: W and NW if made of metal, E or SE if carved in wood, or NE or SW if crafted of an earth material such as clay, porcelain, or terra cotta.

A **dog** symbolizes faithfulness and is valued both as a protector and a scavenger. **Do** put figurines of dogs in the same compass direction that matches its element: W and NW if made of metal, E or SE if carved in wood, or NE or SW if crafted of an earth material such as clay, porcelain, or terra cotta.

Do

❖ Adopt a stray dog if it comes to your home. It is extremely lucky and symbolizes prosperity in abundance coming to you, because the expression "a dog that comes on its own" is an omen of rice (sustenance), fortune or wealth coming to your household.

❖ Place statues of dogs at your door for protection and to keep your prosperity from leaving.

❖ Keep your live pets and their dog house in the rear of the house, even though they may have access to the front.

Dogs (Fu) come in pairs and have traditionally been symbols of protection in front of commercial and residential buildings. They resemble Pekinese dogs with floppy ears and snub noses, and are used outdoors as sentinels just outside the main door, or in back of a house.

The **dragon** is the traditional Chinese symbol of growth, protection, vitality, spring, prosperity, health and new beginnings. In contrast to the negative or evil connotations of the West, it is a very important, benign symbol that represents E, and in feng shui, should always be placed higher than the W. It is also a male or *yang* symbol and therefore should be on the left side. Coupled with the *yin* phoenix, it represents marital happiness and is a popular, traditional wedding symbol.

Living and family rooms, libraries, offices and studies are good places for these mythical creatures where they should be in the E, as well as in the E corner of your desk for harmony and prosperity.

Do

❖ Use dragons when you need the element of E (wood), wood in (S) (fire) or to destroy or overcome earth (SW or NE.)

❖ Put dragons for decorations in your office, especially in E (wood) or carved into your wooden furniture, especially if you were born in the Year of the Dragon.

❖ Choose dragons or pictures of dragons that resemble the qualities of water: slick, shiny, translucent, and the color of the sea, rather than of wood, china, or porcelain, although all materials are acceptable.

❖ First preference is a turquoise or teal-colored dragon, then red, then gold.

❖ Select a grouping of one, two or nine dragons together, or three carved in wood to put in E.

❖ Place your dragon at eye level.

❖ Have your dragon facing any source of clean water such as a lake, river, ocean, beach, waterfall, or fountain.

❖ Combine your dragon with a phoenix, representing a happy, harmonious pairing of partners.

Don't

🙰 Put a dragon, which is a *yang* animal with a lot of energy, in your bedroom which should be restful, peaceful and serene.

🙰 Put your dragon in, facing or near the bathroom or laundry room as these represent dirty water.

Don't

➣ Face your dragon toward N at your home or business.

➣ Put your dragon facing any body of water or a bathroom if there is a room in between.

➣ Buy or use a carpet that has dragon designs on it as these creatures must be able to fly free and would be unable to do so if they are being stepped on.

The **Dragon Tortoise** consists of a dragon head on the body of a tortoise, combining the symbols of growth and strength of the dragon and the longevity and good fortune of the tortoise.

Do

❖ Put them in N as protection as well as to suppress the effects of the direction of the 3 Killings each year.

❖ Indoors, do put them near and facing your front door.

❖ Place one on your desk(either side), especially in the N (tortoise) or E (dragon),but do take care that the figurine does not face you.

The **elephant** symbolizes longevity, power, strength, prudence, wisdom, high moral standards, is one of Buddhism's seven sacred treasures. It is placed in pairs as guardians, standing or kneeling outside or inside a home, flanking its doors. It is also a fertility symbol whose statues are rubbed or stroked to bring children to a family.

Do

❖ Put your elephants in S, the direction associated with long life, E or SE, if they are crafted of wood; in NE or SW if made of porcelain, terra cotta, or china, or a kneeling ceramic one on your altar, in W or NW if made of metal and you want children.

Cunning **fox** is long-lived and often a demonic symbol or a woman. It represents venereal disease and is too fierce an animal to be in your home as it brings a lot of negative energy. It is useful as an image *outdoors* for protection.

Although **frogs** and **toads** are among the noxious creatures, they represent money-making and are considered lucky. These creatures are welcome in homes and gardens as they keep the insect population under control.

A three-legged toad enabled an ancient Chinese official to travel anywhere he wanted, but once in a while, it disappeared down a well, only to be enticed out of hiding with a string of five coins. This toad is depicted with one or three coins in its mouth and symbolizes money making or money coming to you.

In legend, Chang O, the wife of the cruel Chieftain Hou I, stole the Pill of Immortality from her husband to save her people from eternal suffering under his rule. When she was caught red-handed, Chang O swallowed the pill, escaped to the moon, where the gods changed her into a toad whose outline can now be seen in that celestial body. This is the legend told during the Harvest Moon Festival, celebrated on the 15th day of the eighth month on the Chinese lunar calendar.

Do

❖ Place the three-legged toad *on the floor* inside the house, facing *in* as if just entering. You can also put them inside cabinets, under chairs and furniture or diagonally across the room from your front entrance.

❖ Keep a coin in the toad's mouth.

Don't

❧ Put the toad directly *facing* your front door or on an altar as it means that you are facilitating your money going out!

Don't

ॐ Place them in bedrooms, bathrooms, toilets, or kitchens as they are thought to become bad luck and bring negative energy when located in these areas.

The **horse** is the seventh animal in the Chinese zodiac. In the *I Ching*, it represented the female, but later, this animal became *yang* and male. A white horse in Buddhism is the symbol of purity and loyalty. Horses represent the S and wooden ones can be placed there.

Do

❖ Introduce your horse statue or picture into your home or business during the most *yang* period of the day which corresponds to summer, the hours between 11 a.m. to 1 p.m.

❖ Use the horse on your letterhead or log, especially if you are in a business having to do with travel, flight, transportation or trade.

❖ Use one or eight horses which are lucky numbers, but not in a group of five. The horses should look *toward* the house.

❖ Face your horse statue toward S, the most *yang* direction.

❖ Choose a stately animal that is standing or posing calmly with its head level or facing up with dignity, or a galloping horse, symbolizing vigor and strength, not one that is bucking or rearing up (as in fear), especially not in your bedroom because these animals are too *yang*.

Don't

ॐ Place any antique or ceramic horses that came from or are replicas of those originating from Chinese tombs in your house, especially in the wealth, health, marriage areas, or other critical areas. These are *funeral* pieces and therefor connote death and considered unlucky.

The **lion** is the King of Beasts to the Chinese. This magnificent animal is often used in pairs, sitting on their haunches for protection outside homes and businesses, *facing the door*. Lions are sometimes given as a gift for a new home or business, but purchasing your own is acceptable.

Reclining lions can also grace exterior entrances in pairs, as in front of banks, libraries, and other institutional buildings.

Do

❖ Position Chinese lions correctly. Facing out the front of your building, the male with the ball under his paw is on the left (*yang*) side, the female with her lion cub under her paw is on the right (*yin*). He represents the domain of the world at large; hers is offspring and home.

❖ Choose a pair, whichever kind you use, Chinese or Western, that is in proportion in size to the building it graces.

❖ If the lions are small, raise them up higher.

❖ Use lions with great caution as they will cause harm to the persons or businesses they face. A pair of unicorns, fu dogs, elephants or horses are safer substitutes.

❖ Door knockers with lion's heads offers protection to your household if that animal is a part of your family herald or shield.

Don't

☙ Use a lion (or any other animal's) head decorations, e.g., fountains, as it has literally, grave connotations. The exception to this is if a lion's head is a part of your family seal, letterhead, or coat of arms.

☙ Place lions anywhere but on the ground as they are animals of the earth, and not meant to be on roofs, gateposts, or pedestals. The rule of thumb would be not to place a lion's image higher than it would naturally climb or go.

Roosters welcome the new day and its powerful new *yang* energy with its crowing, banishing the night's *yin* energy, replacing it with the pure *yang* of the sun. This bird is very useful to offset the effects of ceiling beams and interior pillars and posts, except in bedrooms.

Do

❖ Use a ceramic rooster to mitigate the dreaded symbol of illness and affliction, the centipede. A "centipede" is a lamp post outside your house or window which has three or more cross posts intersecting the main posts. Imagine the street light or posts looking like a small case t with three or more bars instead of one.

❖ Face the rooster toward such a lamp post, power towers, street light, or beams in your ceiling. The bird's beak should be directly aimed at the offending spot. This measure is the ideal solution for a room that has multiple exposed beams, and a perfect, inconspicuous alternative to hanging a crystal, wind chime, or pair of flutes on every beam!

In feng shui, the **snake** is considered a noxious, treacherous, and wicked creature, although keeping a snakeskin shed by this reptile is thought to bring you riches.

Don't

🐍 Bring snakes as pets or their images into your home

🐍 Injure, harm or kill a snake that takes up residence in or around your house or property. Catch and release it instead for good karma.

Tigers have always been a *yang* symbol of great power, courage, and bravery as it is thought to be the king of wild animals. Any part of this wonderful animal was and is considered powerful medicine and the mythology and legend surrounding tigers have unfortunately contributed to the decimation of its population worldwide. Traditional Asian medicine contends that whichever part of an animal you consume will restore or regenerate the corresponding organs in your body.

Representing West and children, tigers show up on door posts as protection against demons and children wear "tiger caps" as talismans with the animal embroidered on them. In feng shui, the white tiger (west) side of anything should always be lower than the dragon (east) side. They should be positioned *looking away* from the doors they protect.

Do

❖ Activate the children area of your home if you wish to increase your family. Place a stuffed white or yellow tiger or a small picture of a resting or benign tiger with or without cubs, in the west area of your home, especially in the master bedroom.

❖ Put stone or ceramic statues of tigers *outside* your office as guardians.

Don't

᠍᠍⮞ Use images of roaring, attacking, stalking or fierce tigers indoors facing you.

The **tortoise/turtle** represents business success and long life and have been kept in Chinese gardens and monasteries for centuries. To feed or save one by purchasing it from a market where it is sold as food is especially meritorious as it is considered sacred in China. Turtles are one of the celestial animals and are believed to have great protective power. They are kept in homes or ponds in Chinese gardens and are symbols of longevity, good luck, strength, good fortune, and endurance, especially if located in N.

Do

❖ Put *one* in N as they are very auspicious and are the symbol of this direction, in E (wood) or SE (wood) as the element of water nourishes plant life, e.g. element of wood.

Do

❖ Place a ceramic, porcelain, concrete, or clay turtle *in* N *facing* SW or NE.

❖ Keep a turtle, especially black in color, in N. This could be a live terrapin, desert turtle, or a figurine.

❖ Put crystal turtles in N, facing that direction.

❖ Metal turtles of brass, pewter, copper, silver, etc. should face toward W(metal).

❖ Wooden turtles should be facing E (wood) or SE(wood).

❖ Use turtles for ridding the premises of illness in your home.

❖ Hang a picture of a tortoise swimming in water behind you.

❖ Use fresh water turtle shells as an alternative to the bagua mirror for deflecting *sha* energy or poison arrows, and as protection against evil and spirits.

Don't

᠊ Put in any turtles or tortoises (or their images) in S as water puts out fire.

The Chinese **unicorn**, *chi ling*, has almost no resemblance to its European counterpart. This mythical creature may have the attributes of several other animals: the body of a deer, tail of an ox, scales of fish, five cloven toes, and one, two or three fur-covered horns. It is the symbol of goodness, a family with many children or an unending family line. To give a *chi ling* is to bestow good wishes upon someone.

The unicorn represents long life, peace, harmony, protection, and a big family with many children. It is often depicted with a child on its back holding a lotus flower and a flute, and is thought to live a thousand years.

It is believed to appear when a just and wise ruler is governing the country or when a great sage is about to be born. It was last seen at the time Confucius died and has not been sighted since.

Because the unicorn will not step on anything living, including grass or insects, it represents goodness. Kirin, a popular Japanese beer, uses this creature in its logo and on its label.

Do
❖ Put a pair, consisting of a male and a female, of *chi ling* statues for protection outside the front of buildings, flanking the front entrance and to attract good fortune and luck.

The **wolf** is a symbol of cruelty and greed, mistrust and fear. In feng shui, it is not considered a good animal image to have inside your home or office, but is acceptable as a guardian *outside*, such as in the garage.

ANTIQUES

Many people admire and collect antiques, filling their homes and offices with furnishings, clothing, jewelry, and art that have belonged to another person in another time. Because all things absorb the energy of their surroundings, you must recognize that antiques will carry their own, be it positive or negative.

If you know the origin of an antique that you own, use, or wear, e.g., from someone you have known, loved, respected, or admired, you can relax. However, most antiques have been acquired from strangers or places to which you may have traveled, their origins and owners unknown. Antiques in this category must be purified or cleansed *before* they enter your home or you may be introducing unwelcome, unusual or negative energies into your life.

Things to avoid introducing into your home or office are other people's possessions that you purchase from bankruptcy, yard or garage sales, especially if the owners divorced, died, were laid off or fired from their jobs, or experienced other misfortune.

☯ A beautiful blue and white porcelain urn was purchased by Beth, one of my Seattle clients, from a woman who was selling her belongings to raise money to pay attorney's fees for litigation she was involved in. Shortly after, Beth was involved in a lawsuit.

Do

❖ Cleanse antiques with wind (airing outside for a day), water (immersed or sprinkled using sea salt solution, holy or ocean water), fire (smudging with moxibustion stick), sound (bells, singing bowls), or other methods *outside* your home before you bring them inside. Use common sense when choosing the appropriate method so as not to damage your antiques e.g., don't sprinkle water on wooden furniture or clothing, smudge instead.

❖ Be mindful of the original intent, purpose or use of the item. For example, masks may be of the dead or used for burial or exorcism purposes. Statues or replicas of art may have come from tombs, caves, pyramids, cemeteries or temples. The Chinese often used small jade pieces to block the body's openings after death, and the list goes on.

Don't

▪ Bring home or purchase items from estate, garage, yard, etc. sales, without purifying them, nor should you accept gifts or possessions from anyone who is divesting belongings due to calamity, disaster, death or misfortune.

AQUARIUMS

Who among us has not seen a fish tank or aquarium inside or near the front entrance of a Chinese-owned business? The moving, circulating water symbolizes wealth and prosperity for water (and wind) powered the world's sailing vessels to distant shores. In every corner of the world and in every civilization and era, water in the form of rivers, lakes, and oceans has brought trade and commerce, and with them, prosperity.

Do

❖ Put your aquariums in N (business success, career growth) as well as in E or SE for prosperity because they are both wood element directions.

❖ Keep your aquarium about waist-high, not too high or close to the floor.

❖ Use a metal and glass (or acrylic), representing water, aquarium for N as these two elements support each other.

❖ Put eight gold-colored fish with one black in your tank, or just one elegant, slow-moving prosperity fish, an arrowana.

❖ Keep your aquarium and its water clean; the pumps, filters, and other equipment in good working order.

Don't

ᴢ⯈ Put an aquarium in or facing the kitchen, bathroom, or bedroom. The best locations for these mini-environments are living rooms, offices and studies.

ᴢ⯈ Hang pictures of family members, especially those who are deceased, on the wall above your aquarium.

ᴢ⯈ Fret if any of your fish die, for it means that it absorbed something negative that would have happened to you. Replace it as soon as you can to continue that protection.

ASHES

The cremated remains of people and pets emit great amounts of *yin* energy. Remember that feng shui originated from the proper placement of ancestors' grave sites and that there is *yin* feng shui for the dead, and *yang* for you and your *living* family members.

☆ My friends Gary and Lillian kept their beloved dog's ashes in an urn in their bedroom and then wondered why her health suffered! One of our relatives kept the ashes of his departed wife in his downstairs family room and couldn't understand why he never prospered!

Do
❖ Bury the ashes of your departed loved ones away from your home in a cemetery or at a distance from your house, only if it is legal to do so.

❖ Keep the grave site clean and swept of any debris.

❖ Try to find a location that has good feng shui which requires the grave being on high ground, nestled into a hill, with a wide view, preferably of water, in front. After all, the origin of this practice was for the proper placement of ancestors' grave sites.

Don't
☜ The ashes of any person or pet do not belong inside your home. Do not keep them on the premises as they represent death.

AWARDS

Do
❖ Hang your diplomas, awards, kudos, trophies, and other accolades and commendations on the south wall of your office or home as this direction represents fame and fortune.

Do

❖ Put up pictures of you with the rich and famous, or gifts from them and other celebrities, in the S.

BAGUA (Ba-gua, pa kua)

Any octagon is called a **bagua**, as are busybodies, *yentas*, meddling, or even superstitious people! In feng shui, this eight-sided shape is used for protection, divination, fortune telling, and other purposes. (see figure on pages 148 and 156)

The two most important uses for the *bagua* in feng shui is as a guide as to where to put what, and in the use of the eight-sided mirror, called a bagua mirror.

In both the Compass School and the Black Sect Tantric Tibetan Buddhism School of feng shui, the bagua is placed on the floor plan of the room, office, or house. Also in both schools, the octagon is stretched or elongated accordingly to accommodate the different shapes of rooms, houses, apartments, gardens, properties, etc.

When there is a negative space, e.g., no structural presence, it is a "missing corner/area" that needs to be replaced metaphysically with the use of lights, rocks, overhangs, mirrors, etc. And thirdly, in both schools, you enhance or activate the desired aspects of your life by deliberately putting something there.

From the following diagrams, you can see how differently each school   handles a particular space and why there is so much confusion about how to use and practice feng shui. Compare the two schools' treatments of the identical floor plan, and you will see the contrast between them.

In the Compass School (below), theoretically, the eight areas of any room in a basically rectangular or square space, correspond to the same walls/areas in adjoining rooms. Thus, N-NE-E-SE-S-SW-W-NW will **always** be in N-NE-E-SE-S-SW-W-NW in any room, according to your compass.

COMPASS SCHOOL

SE	S	SW	SE	S	SW
E	*Kitchen*	W	E	*Dining Room*	W
NE	N	NW	NE	N	NW

The following list provides the eight compass directions and what they represent in the Compass School of feng shui: North = Career, business success, black, winter, water/metal, tortoise, 1; North East = Knowledge, wisdom, self-development, success in school, turquoise/tan, winter becoming spring, earth/fire, 8; East = Family life, health, nutrition, harmony, prosperity, green, spring, wood/water, dragon, 3; South East = Wealth, prosperity, abundance, green/purple, spring becoming summer, wood/water, 4; South = Fame, fortune, longevity, festivity, joy, fire/wood, red, summer, bird, 9; South West = Marriage, mother, relationships, love, romance, spouse, yellow/white/pink/red, summer becoming autumn, earth/fire, 2; West = Children, children's fame, creativity, white, autumn, tiger, metal/earth, 7; North West = Supportive and helping people, international trade and travel, interests outside the home, father, autumn becoming winter, metal/earth,grey/metallics, 6.

In the BSTB School of feng shui, the various areas of your *aspirations and accomplishments* will change from room/space to room/space, depending on the location of most frequently-used entrance to the room, for that is your reference point. Therefore, the wealth area, for example, changes from one spot to another in adjoining rooms, due to the locations of the entrances to those rooms.

BLACK (Hat) SECT TIBETAN BUDDHIST SCHOOL

The list below provides the eight areas of any space (beginning at the entrance and moving clockwise) **according to the BSTB School of feng shui**, where each is located, and the aspirations each area represents.

> Front Center (entrance looking in)=Career, business, work, water, fountains, black/white objects
>
> Left Front=Knowledge, self-development, wisdom, success, goals, books, personal health/growth items, blue/green/black

Left Center=Family, health, ancestors, relatives, family
heirlooms, souvenirs, shrines to ancestors, photos,
blue/green
Left Rear=Weath, prosperity, abundance, material things
fountains, fish, things of value, aquariums, banner,
red/purple/blue/green
Center Rear (across from main entrance)=Fame, fortune
awards, diplomas, fireplace, candles, red/green
Right Rear=Marriage, relationships, romance
Right Center = Children, creativity, round, metal,
arts/crafts, toys, games, white/metallics
Right Front=Supportive and helping people, religious icons,
travel, friends, black/white/grey

There are several types of **bagua mirrors**; each is different and has a unique purpose. Generally, they are flat, concave, and convex, and each has a different degree of power.

Do

❖ Remember that we use these reflective aids, primarily for
protection, and only as a last resort and never to harm anyone.

❖ Always hang *bagua* mirrors on the EXTERIOR of your home or
office, <u>never</u> on the inside.

❖ Use a flat, eight-sided or round mirror for common problems
such as for garbage cans or dumpsters, barking dogs, etc.

❖ Use the colored *bagua* mirror for reflecting back *sha* (killing)
energy originating from a straight road, tunnel, bridge, or corner
of a building, or unpleasant neighbors. This mirror is a octagon-
shaped piece of wood with a round, flat mirror at its centre. It
is painted red (protection), bordered in green (for prosperity,
strength and vitality), and has the eight trigrams of the *I Ching*
stamped in gold surrounding the mirror. The trigrams give this
neutral mirror its power and because it sends back the negative

energy toward its origin, be careful how and where you use it. After I installed them for several of my clients, their undesirable neighbors have actually moved away after their negative energy was aimed back at them.

❖ Use the concave (bowl-shaped) *bagua* mirror facing *sha* energy which you want to be absorbed into the mirror and not reflected back to the origin of the *sha*, e.g., a school at the end of a straight road aimed toward your house. It works quietly without harm to anyone or anything.

❖ Exercise great prudence and caution when using the convex (protruding or curving *out*) mirror as it reflects whatever images received and sends them back out again, possibly harming someone.

BAR

A wet bar inside or outside of your house is best located in N (water) or W (metal and socializing area).

BATHROOM

In feng shui, the placement of the bathroom is very important as it is the place of cleansing, the origin of unpleasant odors and human waste, and their disposal. Bathrooms are also where much of the water drains away from your home, so preferably they should not be located in your important areas, e.g. health, wealth. The best direction for bathrooms, tubs, and showers is in the N whose element is water, used for washing, cleansing, and purifying.

In general, it not a good idea to spend tremendous amounts of time in or money on this area of the home. Keep the décor commensurate with the function: simple! It makes no sense to spend lots of your hard-earned money on this area. Your resources are better concentrated on more important areas of your home such as the master bedroom, kitchen, study, or office.

Do

❖ Have your toilet with a door to close it off - remember the origin name for the toilet was water *closet*?

▪ You can also hang a wind chime made of an earth material such as terra cotta or porcelain, or one that has five *solid clay* rods to "dam" your business success and career from going down the drain if your toilet is in the N.

▪ Hang a mirror on the outside of the toilet door if the toilet happens to be in the wealth area of your home or office, as well as a wind chime in the window.

▪ Install a simple, round or octagonal mirror above the outside door frame of the toilet if it is located in the wealth area of SE.

☯ This is what I did, and within 24 hours, the producer from the Oprah Winfrey show called me to be a guest on OPRAH.

Don't

▪ Pick a house in which the bathroom is located above the front entrance as this portends major calamity to the family.

▪ Choose a home in which the bathroom, and particularly the toilet, is located in the SE, the wealth and prosperity areas of E, S or SE, or in SW which is the area of marriage and relationships.

▪ Put a toilet across from your kitchen, main entrance, or at the center of the house.

home or past the front horizontal line of the main entrance. If it
does, your wealth will flush and drain out. This predicament
can be mitigated by painting the bathroom any earth color,
such as yellow, using accessories made from porcelain, clay,
china, or terra cotta, and using earth colors in the towels, e.g.,
yellow, orange, brown, tan, or beige. All of these represent earth
suppressing or holding back water. You can also put a large
stone on top of the closed toilet seat cover and stop using that
particular washroom. By using the element of earth, you are
damming the flow of water (wealth) out of your home.

BED

Because we spend one third of our lives sleeping, bed
placement is critical for good rest and recharging our energies.
Sleeping with your head pointed toward one of your four best
directions ensures terrific rest. Many feng shui masters in Taiwan,
however, advise that your *feet* should point toward one of those
four because when you sit up in bed before you swivel to rise, you
will <u>face</u> one of the beneficial directions, thus receiving beneficial
energy. I have used *both* systems with great success, so experiment
to find which (head or feet pointing) gives you the optimum sleep
and rest.

Do

❖ Position your bed so that it is not in line with the entrance to
your bedroom, and especially if the feet point toward that
entrance. This "death position" is almost universal as the bodies
of those who die at home are carried out of a room or house feet
first.

❖ Choose bedding and linens that are solids in color, but if they
have patterns, avoid geometric, angular designs which emanate
negative energy and disturb your rest.

❖ Put your bed in one of the positions shown in the following diagrams:

Bed Placement

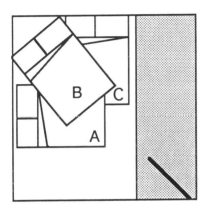

(Do not place bed in shaded area.)

Do

❖ Use a headboard that is constructed of wood, metal or foam, matching its shape with the element of the direction that the room is in: arches and round shapes for W (metal) and NW (metal); rectangles and squares for E (wood) and SE (wood); curvy, wavy or irregular shapes for N (water); and triangular shapes for S (fire).

Don't

ℨ Put the head of a bed against a window unless there is a solid headboard, curtain, drapes, blinds, or shutters are there to block off the window.

ℨ Place the bed under a beam. If this cannot be helped, install a false ceiling with fabric or construct a ceiling over the bed, or hang wind chimes, flutes or red fringe on the beam. Beams represent separation if they happened to occur between a bed's occupants, and a shortened life or health problems in the area of the occupant's body they bisect.

ℨ Use twin beds shoved together or twin box springs under your king-size mattress if you are sharing your bed with someone. These arrangements symbolize a split in your relationship with that person. If you have twin box springs, tie the adjoining legs together securely with red cord so that they will not split apart.

⤳ Place the head of your bed on a wall shared with a toilet on the other side.

⤳ Position a bed on the short wall of a room with a pitched ceiling as the energy will press down on the occupant.

⤳ Use round windows, skylights or unusual ceilings in a bedroom.

⤳ Move the bed when your wife is pregnant.

BEDROOM

One of the most important rooms in feng shui, the master bedroom ideally should be past and behind the center horizontal line of the house, not in the front of the house. SW, the area of marriage, spouse, and relationships is the best area of the house for the master bedroom.

Because sleeping is a *yin* activity, your bedroom should minimize *yang* colors such as a lot of gold or red that stimulate your energy resulting in poor rest or sleep.

Do
❖ Construct a false ceiling or one of fabric to hide any beams in your bedroom. Remember that in feng shui: . If you can't see it, it's not there.

❖ Create a safe haven for sleeping, rest, intimacy and making love, and recharging your spirit and body.

❖ Remove as much electronic equipment from your bedroom as possible, especially televisions, VCRs, stereos, computers, etc., all of which emit electromagnetic energy which is detrimental to good rest, health and fertility.

❖ Keep your bedroom free of clutter and minimize furniture so that *chi* can flow smoothly throughout the room..

Do

❖ Take notice of the view that greets you when you awaken. What's outside your bedroom window - a lamppost, church spire, neighboring rooftops or corners of your neighbor's house? Are any of them poison arrows disturbing your sleep or rest? Take corrective measures to offset them. (See **BAGUA** and **MIRRORS**)

❖ Use a concave *bagua* mirror to absorb any of these poison, killing arrows aimed at you.

❖ Avoid sleeping in any bedroom situated above a garage which channels the noxious fumes from the automobiles stored within up to the room's occupants, affecting good health.

❖ Use plants and flowers in an ill or convalescing person's room to introduce healing *yang* energy there.

❖ Watch the placement of desks, shelves, cabinets, wardrobes, other furniture and architectural features so that their corners do not point toward the bed.

❖ Cleanse the energy of the room several times a year with wind (airing), sound (music, bells, singing bowls, chimes, xylophone, etc.) fire (smudging with Chinese herb stick or incense), or water (sprinkling or misting all corners and walls with purified or holy water.) Use the form of energy cleansing that matches the oncoming season: water for spring and winter, fire for summer, and metal, sound instruments for autumn.

❖ The best times for cleansing is a new moon, solstices (March 21, June 21, September 21 or December 21), or whenever you feel the atmosphere in your space feels heavy, stale or hostile, such as after an argument, illness or death on the premises.

❖ It is imperative to air out a room or house thoroughly for at least an hour after smudging by opening all the doors and windows so that the absorbed negative energy is drawn out and dispersed to the outdoors.

❖ Close any bathroom doors and toilet seat covers if a bathroom leads into your bedroom. This simple habit can ensure a good night's sleep.

Don't

↝ Put any altars or deities in the bedroom. However, if there is no other spot in your home for them, locate them *past* the foot of the bed.

↝ Use too much red, gold or other strong *yang* colors that will cause poor sleep. Remember, do everything in moderation strive for balance- the golden rules of feng shui.

↝ Use any plants that have sharp foliage, e.g., cactus, or too many plants as they emit too much *yang* energy for quality rest.

↝ Use electric blankets or water beds. The first generates electromagnetic currents and the latter is believed to cause arthritis, muscle pain and joint problems.

↝ Have any cactus or other plants that have pointed foliage as they send forth small arrows of *sha* energy.

↝ Sleep with your bed in direct line with the room's entrance with your feet pointing toward it. This is the death position and those who expire at home are carried out of the room feet first in many cultures. If there is no alternative to bed placement, be sure to close any doors at night, especially if they lead to a bathroom.

↝ Have any water features such as fountains or aquariums in your bedroom as these are considered unlucky there, leading to loss of your wealth.

ᴈᴗ Occupy any bedroom which is in direct line with a straight road. If any automobile headlights shine at or into the bedroom at night, use the room for exercise, storage, sewing, computer, game, or other non-sleeping purposes instead.

BELLS

Bells are especially useful in feng shui for cleansing a person's or an area's energy, and attract prosperity when hung on the <u>outside</u> doorknobs of the entrances of homes and businesses.

Choose bells that are new, with a wooden handle for your cleansing activities, cleaned by wiping after each use and stored in W as it is the element of metal. Brass and silver bells are the best and in the sounds or tones that appeal to you.

Bells that have been used in temples or churches are not advised to be brought into your home as they have absorbed the energies of the people who have come to the temples to seek absolution of their transgressions.

☆ A close relative of mine purchased a huge temple bell from China and despite warnings from other family members to get rid of it, had it installed as a prominent decoration right next to his front door. Tragedy and misfortunes soon followed, beginning with a freak accident that killed his oldest son.

☆ The business of one of my clients declined after she brought home a Thai temple bell and put it on her living room coffee table for decoration.

You see, the word *joong* is the homonym for "end or conclusion," so the expression *soong jung*, literally, "to give a clock/bell [end]" represents the ringing of temple bells at funerals in China, much like the Western custom of ringing a town's or city's bells for like occasions.

It is for this reason you should never give a bell, clock or anything with a clock's face as a gift to your Chinese friends and relatives because it has an unlucky connotation. This is akin to our not giving a gift of a pair of scissors, a set of knives or swords to someone as it symbolizes severing a relationship or a life.

On the other hand, bells are traditionally sounded to accompany happy news or tidings. Two small, <u>new</u> bells hanging on the *outside* door handle or knob of your business likewise signal the arrival of customers, therefore your prosperity entering.

Do
❖ Use those with pleasant tinkling sounds for activating *yang* energy in your home or business.

❖ String one or three bells together with auspicious red ribbon, thread, or cord and hang them on your door knob or handle or above your door so they sound joyously when guests and customers enter.

❖ When hung on the outside door handle or knob of the main entrance to your home as well as the outside doorknobs of rooms, bells attract good luck and good fortune and keep the prosperity that you enjoy *inside* your home.

❖ Hang a pair, or six or seven tinkling bells with red cord on your door or doorknob, especially if you are a business, to signal the entrance of customers to your premises.

❖ Bells are best located in the metal areas of W, NW, or across from the entrance, never in E or SE, both wood areas.

❖ Buy and use *new* bells for your cleansing work.

❖ Ring a bell in the corners of a room to clear stagnant or stale energy.

❖ Give your bell in a single, firm shake above a person's head
   and then holding it about six inches away, trace the person's
   body down from head to toe to cleanse his/her energy.

❖ Match the material that your bell is made of with the element of
   the direction of the room or that which the main entrance faces.

Don't
☞ Introduce bells that have been used inside temples or churches
   into your home or property as they have absorbed the energy of
   those with sin and you'll introduce that negative energy into your
   home.

BIRDS

In Chinese culture and in feng shui, birds figure prominently
and with great deal of symbolism, almost all positive. Birds belong
in S and SW when in pairs.

It is preferable to have paintings, statues, figurines, and
other art of birds that are uncaged. A cage, with or without a bird,
represents entrapment and loss of freedom, and limiting your fame
and fortune, therefore, bird cages are not good feng shui. However
if you want to use them as plant holders, that is acceptable.

The **crane** has been long associated with good fortune,
wealth, wisdom, and long life for the patriarch and matriarch of a
family. It is believed to carry souls to heaven, live up to 600 years,
and is often found in pairs, under a pine tree, another symbol of
longevity. **Do** put a pair of metal cranes in a water element in your
garden if it is in the N, for water and metal make a powerful and
beautiful combination. Add metal to water, but not vice versa, for
metal creates water, but water combined with metal, rusts it.

Another symbol of long life is the **dove** or **pigeon**, a gift of
which sculpted in jade was given to bestow best wishes for good

health and continued longevity. If carved in wood, **do** put doves in S for long life and to fuel the element of fire there.

A pair of **Mandarin ducks**, a male and a female, represent marital devotion, fidelity, and happiness, because they are attached to each other. When separated, the birds are believed to pine away to the point of death. If you wish to improve your relationship with your partner, **do** put these symbols in the SW, the corresponding area for this aspect of your life.

Eagles/Hawks are birds of prey and therefore not good feng shui indoors, but flying eagles and hawks can represent soaring success, especially if the picture or sculpture is in S. **Do** put statues of them *outside* for protection away from your house down a driveway or flanking gates. Hang a picture of a hawk or eagle in near your back or garage door for protection. **Don't** display statues, images or pictures of these predatory birds with their victims clasped in their talons, hovering about their dead or half-eaten prey, or facing you directly in an attack mode.

Wild **geese,** which always fly in pairs, are messengers of good news and represent the married state. A pair of these is a good symbol to place in the relationship and marriage area of your bedroom, SW.

Lovebirds and figurines of a pair of lovebirds are the ideal accessory in the SW romance and marriage corner of your home, garden or bedroom.

Magpies are harbingers of joy, happiness, and festivity, and are good luck omens, for they always bring happy news. If they set up reisdence near your home, trees or under the eaves, great good fortune is sure to follow. Use these birds in your decoration and placed them in S.

The most common, celebrated bird in Chinese culture is the **phoenix**, symbol of *yin*, the female, and the head of all feathered creatures. It is composed of several different animals: the swallow, fowl, snake, fish, crane, dragon, tortoise, and a mandarin drake. Five colors, representing the five virtues are found in its feathers.

Seen in art motives everywhere, this mythical creature, like the *chi ling*, is believed only to appear when China is governed by a just, reasonable, and fair ruler, or during peaceful and prosperous times. It personifies everything good and beautiful, and first appeared around the time of Confucius' birth.

Shown alone, the phoenix symbolizes *yang* energy and opportunities. When embroidered or depicted on red bridal wear, tapestries, coverlets, bedspreads, clothing and decorations, the phoenix appears on the right (when you are facing it), with its companion, the dragon, representing the man, on the left, and a small flock of smaller birds fly in its wake to attend to it. Thus coupled, the phoenix then becomes *yin* to the dragon's *yang* energy.

Do
❖ Use this beautiful bird in any form in your SW area to attract happy relationships and marriage.

❖ Place the phoenix in higher spots in your household, in comparison to the dragon's eye level location.

Sometimes the **pheasant,** another symbol of beauty, substitutes for the phoenix, which represents south, sun, fire, and the continuation of the family line. **Do** put the phoenix or pheasant, in the S for fame and fortune. One carved in wood is doubly powerful as the wood element nourishes the fire element.

The **swallow** which builds its nests under the eaves of buildings portends approaching success or a lucky change in the fortunes or affairs of the occupant of the premises. Its image is found in Chinese art and clothing. **Do** place the swallow in E (wood) or S (fire) to enhance your good fortune and prosperity.

BONSAI

The practice manipulating the growth of trees originated in China. The dwarfed, miniature plants were treasured as they represented a microcosm of the world. Bonsai are beautiful to look at, but the trees' stunted growth is not good feng shui as they represent limits on your development, possibilities and opportunities. For this reason, do not give these plants as gifts. (They are best kept outdoors where they thrive.)

BOOKS

One of the eight symbols of the scholar, books can be used to stimulate NE, the area of knowledge, wisdom, and scholarly success. Because education is so venerated in China, books such as the classic *I Ching*, the Book of Changes, were wrapped in red silk and kept under one's pillow, or in a nearby room or library to deter evil spirits.

Do
❖ Put books in a closed bookcase if possible to eliminate the negative energy caused by the edges of the shelves directed at anyone occupying the room.

❖ Use scholarly books to improve success in school by placing them in the NE area of a child's bedroom.

❖ Put college handbooks from the schools of choice in NE to ensure academic success.

❖ Encourage your child to study in the NE area or face his or her
   best direction at home or that area of his/her bedroom to
   facilitate learning, wisdom and scholarly success.

❖ Remove pornographic, violent, warlike, depressing, or lewd
   posters and publications from a young person's bedroom if you
   wish him/her success in school and life.

   ☆ I advised the removal of the cheesecake "bikini-girl"
posters from the bedroom wall of a client's son, and the young man
went on to study and graduate from a prestigious East Coast
university.

Don't
☙ Use glass shelves in N, wooden shelves in SW, NE, or the center
of   your room.

BROOMS
   Brooms symbolize wisdom and insight, and are used before
the Chinese New Year to create the proverbial "clean slate" for the
coming year. They are then put away before midnight so they do
not inadvertently sweep away the good luck of the incoming new
year.

Do
❖ Keep brooms, mops, trash cans, and other cleaning tools,
   supplies and equipment, etc. out of sight when not in use.

❖ Keep a broom standing on its handle outside your front
   door to deter strangers, burglars and undesirable guests during
   the night, but remember to put it away during the day.

Don'ts
☙ Leave cleaning supplies in the dining room as they symbolize
   the "cleaning out" of one's income, good health, nutrition
   and prosperity.

Don't

🍃 Leave a broom out behind you if you are gambling in case your luck gets swept away.

🍃 Brooms should not be kept in the room of a dying person as they are believed to sweep away life.

BUDDHA

Because Buddha is a significant and revered deity, his image should be regarded, treated, and handled with reverence and respect. There are many statues of Buddha and to activate your prosperity, be sure to choose the right one!

All other religious icons and holy art should also be treated as such by placing them in a location above the height of the tallest person who may enter a room. It is very unlucky to house any altars in a room where there is regular sexual activity.

☆ The Busy Bee Market is a small, family-owned grocery store with practically bare shelves and customers lining out the door during every lunch hour. The market's limited but popular offerings are its excellent hot and cold sandwiches and drinks sold from two refrigerator cases. On top of one of them is a garish, gold-colored four-feet high carved wooden, laughing Buddha, facing the front entrance and overlooking the cash register where the owners do little but stand and ring up their sales daily.

Do

❖ Pick a laughing Buddha for your home or business. He is the cheerful, chubby chap with a pot belly, carrying a gourd or a bag hanging from a staff held over one shoulder, and sometimes an ingot in one hand. The bag contains your troubles and problems which he has collected and contained for you.

❖ Position your laughing Buddha up on a high shelf and so that he is angled to face the front door of your home or business. This spot can be behind the register or on a back wall if it isn't too far away from the main entrance to your business.

❖ Use the largest size of Buddha you like, keeping it in proportion to the size of the room in which it's located.

❖ Decorate with a Buddha that has children climbing all over him, which represents an abundance of good fortune coming from heaven.

❖ Position your Buddha diagonally across from the door, facing it.

❖ Keep your Buddha at the same height or higher than the occupants of a room, raised if possible, not on the ground where you would look down on the Buddha.

❖ Obtain a new Buddha and invite him into your home. Beware of introducing used or antique statues or figurines, especially from temples from any country, into your possession. Be sure to cleanse or purify such deities before bringing them into your home or business for they may carry unwanted, negative energy.

Don't

☛ Place a Buddha statue on the ground, but rather up high, ensconced inside an altar or on a pedestal.

☛ Use a reclining Buddha in a business or place it on the ground.

☛ Put Buddha in a dining room or bedroom where there is regular sexual activity.

BURNER/STOVE

The burners/stoves in your home represent the prosperity of the family so they are of utmost importance. The more burners you have in your kitchen, the more wealth you have, and it is critical that they should be kept clean and in good working order at all times.

Some developers have been installing a separate wok kitchen away from the main stove, figuring that if the stove symbolizes prosperity, surely two of them would double a family's wealth. In fact, two kitchens *divide* the wealth. An increase in the number of burners on the stove top is the proper way to achieve increased prosperity.

Generally, when you are standing at your stove, you should be facing either E (wood) or S (fire) as in ancient civilizations, humans burned wood to create fire with which to cook their food. Knowing your best directions, you should have your stove *across* from your 4th best direction.

Do

❖ Choose a home that has your burners/stove with a wall behind it, rather than one that has the stove on an island or peninsula. The wall provides solid, continual support to the prosperity of your family. If you are not planning to remodel soon, you can use decorative stove covers or a three-paneled aluminum "screen" (found in kitchenware shops for limiting the oil splatters when deep frying) to create a "wall."

❖ Avoid having the stove and the sink share the same counter close together, side by side or, causing a clash of elements, as water destroys fire.

❖ In Black Sect Tantric Tibetan Buddhist form of feng shui, it is acceptable and even encouraged to install mirrors on the wall behind the burners to double your money. However, many Compass School feng shui practitioners advise that no mirrors should be in the kitchen or bedroom as this causes friction and discord in these rooms. Since these two practices contradict each other, you can hang a metal wind chime with five hollow rods over your stove instead!

Don't
📚 Have the stove and the sink located directly across from each other if one is on an island or peninsula, as this is a clash of the elements: water putting out/destroying fire, which represents the family's livelihood and wealth. If they are positioned not directly across from either, e.g., offset, then they can be across the aisle.

CALLIGRAPHY

Calligraphy is one of the traditional arts of China and is revered for the spirit or *chi* that emanates from it. Because the written form of the Chinese language is comprised of strokes created with a brush, the ability to capture the denotation of a word while at the same time forming a character that was aesthetically pleasing was greatly admired.

To own and display the works of a great calligrapher, artist, or official was a source of pride, with each owner adding his signature chop (stamp) to the artwork to verify ownership, thus adding to its value.

Do
❖ Display calligraphy of prosperity, good luck and fortune in the appropriate areas of your home or office: E, SE, N, and S.

❖ Hang Chinese scrolls with inspirational poetry or verses in N.

❖ Hang motivational messages in NE.

CANDLES

Nothing surpasses candles to activate S, the one area of the fire element, or for creating more of the earth element. No mystery or mysticism here - just envision the Hawaiian Islands and their awesome volcanoes, generating tons of lava oozing out to the Pacific, giving birth to new islands, e.g., earth.

Fire symbolizes fame, fortune, longevity, joy and festivity, and if you want these in your life, candles will do the job for you! But don't forget that in the generative cycle of the elements, fire creates earth, the elements representing relationships, love, marriage, motherhood, as well as knowledge, intelligence, scholarly success, and self-development.

Burning beeswax candles can eliminate the impurities and add lots of healthful and healing negative ions to the air. These help to purify a space or help you to relax and improve your sleep. Use mists instead of scented paraffin candles (which deplete the oxygen) before sleep in a bedroom.

When using candles in S, SW, or NE, remember: don't just put them in these spots, wrapped in cellophane and collecting dust - you have to light them too! It is the flame that creates the *yang* energy which activates the fire and earth areas.

Do
❖ Place red, blue or purple candles in S to stimulate celebrity and fame, fortune, reputation, happiness and festivity.

❖ Add white, yellow, orange, pink or red candles to reinforce SW, the area of love, marriage, relationships, motherhood, and romance.

❖ Put blue, green, or turquoise candles in NE to support this area

of knowledge, scholarly success, wisdom, experience, and self-development.

Don't
▪ Use candles in any of the metal element areas of W or NW for fire melts metal.

CASH REGISTER

The cash register of a business should be placed carefully as it represents its prosperity. Take careful note of the whereabouts and placement of cash registers at successful restaurants and businesses, Chinese and non-Chinese alike. You will notice a definite trend.

Do

❖ Place your cash register on the *yang* or left side (facing out), near the front entrance.

❖ Install mirrors around the cash register to double your money intake.

❖ Place a prosperity, jade plant, or other live plant near your cash register. Cut flowers create *yang* energy, but discard them when they wilt.

❖ If you use a cash box, paint it red (prosperity, fortune) or black (business success).

❖ Keep the counters around the register clean and clear of clutter, especially applications for credit card displays, and other solicitations. The exception is a collection box for charity that you support which encourages your customers to share their abundance which is very good karma.

❖ You may put one attractive, quick-selling point of purchase item on your counter.

❖ Tape a lucky red money envelope with three silver dollars or a high denomination bill inside, or Chinese coins tied with red cord or ribbon to the bottom of the drawer with the *yang* side facing out.

❖ Hang prosperity images such as that of an arrowana, dragon gold ingots, Chinese junk, three gods of prosperity, God of Wealth seated on the back of a tiger, wish-fulfilling ox, etc. behind the cash register. If you don't want to bother with the care and maintenance of live fish, you can follow the example I saw at a Chinese restaurant. A four-color, full-size photograph of an arrowana was hanging on the wall above the cash register!

❖ If you have a laughing Buddha (see **BUDDHA**), place it on a shelf near or behind your cash register, facing the door, higher than the tallest person in the room.

❖ Put the three-legged frogs (facing in as if they were bringing in wealth) or lions *on the ground*, where they belong, not up high.

Don't

☛ Position your cash box or register under any lowered, pitched or sloped ceiling or a beam as it will suppress your wealth.

☛ Have any displays of cigarettes, candy, gum, etc. hanging over your cash register, as these represent suppressing the profits.

☛ Clutter up the area around your cash register with telephone books, old receipts, papers, etc. Put everything away inside a drawer or closed cabinet nearby, or get rid of it.

COINS

Coins symbolize wealth and good fortune and can be used as decoration and to attract more prosperity to your home or business. The best kind to use are ancient Chinese coins that are round (representing heaven) with a square hole (representing earth) in the center. When you are holding a coin, you are holding a little bit of heaven and earth.

`If you are unable to find or purchase ancient Chinese coins, silver dollars will suffice, in multiples of threes, sixes, or nines, *never* in fives.

Do

❖ Tie three coins together with red cord or string and hang them on the inside of your main door to your home or office, as well as the outside doorknobs or handles of interior doors. This gesture keeps your prosperity *inside* your home and are especially effective if your front entrance faces one of the metal directions of W or NW.

❖ Put two or three silver dollars inside a lucky, red money envelope, or wrap them in red paper to tape to your fax machine, telephone, copy machine, inside your wallet, and cash box or register.

❖ Wear nine Chinese coins in any combination of jewelry for good fortune: earrings, bracelet, brooch, ring, etc.

❖ Use the symbol of two Chinese coins, especially over the door frame of your business, for prosperity. My publisher, Pacific Heritage Books, cleverly replaces the oo in "Books" with two overlapping coins in its logo to resemble two Chinese coins with the square holes at their centers.

❖ Wear nine coins together or other coin shapes such as jade doughnuts or disks with holes in their centers. Jade or other greenstone, especially if new, is a traditional form of protection and good fortune.

Don't

❧ Hang any coins on your *back* door as that represents your money *leaving* the premises!

COLORS

Throughout human civilization, color has had symbolic power in every culture around the globe. It has represented rank, status, power, and a range of emotions. In China, the imperial color was yellow and only the emperor and his family could wear it. His royal weavers and craftsmen were charged with the responsibility of creating exquisite and fabulous designs with the exclusive, five-clawed dragon on garments, tapestries, embroideries, and other fabrics. Everyone else could only use the four-clawed dragons for decoration, and was punished by death if caught using the imperial symbol or color.

The primary colors to the Chinese are red, yellow, blue (and green), white, and black, always brilliant, and the outlines dominant.

Aqua/Turquoise (*ching*) represents the NE (knowledge, wisdom, self development, experience) and E (dragon, wood, family, harmony, health, nutrition, growth, vitality, prosperity, youth, spring). It is the color of the sky after rain and that of the ocean.

Black symbolizes N (water, tortoise, business success, career, new beginnings, mourning, evil, consequences of man, guilt). **Don't** use this in bedrooms, or on walls or ceilings in any room, as it is a *yin* color, or combined with yellow, or in SW (earth) or NE (earth).

Brown/Beige/Tan is used to represent the element of wood and E (spring, youth, prosperity, family, harmony, nutrition, strength, growth, vitality). The Syrians use this color for mourning as it represents fallen leaves, e.g., death.

Blue, especially ultramarine or reflex blue in printer's language, is the deep, purplish blue found in the tiles of Japanese rooftops. It can be used to represent N (water, business success, career) and enhances E(wood, family, harmony, growth, health). **Don't** use it in

SW (earth) or NE (earth), or wear it in a ribbon or bow in your hair as this is one of the traditional Chinese mourning symbols.

Gold (metallic) is used to symbolize W (metal, children, children's fame, creativity) and to enhance N(water, business success, career) as well as NW (metal, supportive people, trade, travel, interests outside the home). **Do** use it to represent prosperity and wealth. **Don't** use it in bedrooms as it destroys health and harmony, in E (wood, health, prosperity, family), or SE (wood, wealth, prosperity)

Gold(non-metallic) is the symbol of the earth and SW (marriage, motherhood, spouse, love, relationships) and can be used in NE, (wisdom, knowledge, scholarly success) another earth sign. **Do** use it to enhance W (metal) or NW (metal).**Don't** use it in N (water, business success, career).

Green is the color of E (wood, dragon, health, harmony, prosperity, youth, growth, spring) and of SE (wood, wealth, prosperity). **Do** use it to enhance S (fire, fame, fortune, joy, festivity, protection from evil.) **Don't** use it in SW (earth) or NE (earth.)

Gray is the color representing NW (metal, supportive people, benefactors, mentors, international trade, trips, travel, interests outside the home.) **Do** use it also in W (metal) or N (water. **Don't** use it in E (wood) or SE (wood).

Orange is an earth color and is used in SW (motherhood, romance, love, relationships, marriage). **Do** use it to enhance W (metal) and NW (metal.) **Don't** use it in N (water.)

Peach is the color particularly for use by single women to attract a good husband. **Do** use it liberally in your *unmarried* daughter's bedroom so she will marry well. If you can find peonies or pictures or paintings of this color, put them outside her bedroom.

Don't use peach in your bedroom if you are already married, as this is the hue that will activate your partner's roving eye or heart, causing infidelity. Put this color in your living or dining room instead.

Pink represents romance, love, and marriage. This is an excellent color for use in any single woman's bedroom, and is especially powerful in S (fire) or SW (relationships.)

Purple is the color of knowledge and wisdom, intelligence, wealth, and spirituality. It was also an imperial color for the Chinese. Do use purple in the E (wood, harmony, prosperity, family, health), or in the SE (wealth, prosperity.) It is a substitute color for green to represent good fortune.

Next to black, **Red** is the most powerful, *yang* color in Chinese culture. It represents S (fire, fame, fortune, joy, festivity, longevity, summer, passion, protection from bad luck and evil.)

Do
❖ Use red in S in any form, especially red birds, thus combining two symbols of this compass direction.

❖ Newlyweds, brides, people celebrating their birthdays, temple doors, baby blankets, firecrackers, embroideries, tapestries, etc. are clothed in and surrounded by this color.

❖ Tie two red cords or ribbons on the inside of your bedroom door handle or knob if you'd like to attract a serious partner to your life.

❖ Red hearts and silk flowers are excellent to put in the SW (relationships, marriage, love, romance, motherhood) or S (fire, fame, fortune, long life, reputation, prosperity.)

Don't

☙ Use too much of this color (bright, lacquer or firecracker red) in a bedroom as it is too active and *yang*, thus disturbing the occupant's rest.

☆ Several years ago, I met a highly-successful attorney at a social function.

"I meet and date a lot of men," she told me, "but after a short while, lose interest and can't keep the relationship going. Give me a couple of quick fixes so I can find a husband." Having determined from her hastily-drawn sketch that her bedroom door was located in the SW and therefore promoted a constant in-and-out flow of men and relationships in her life, I advised her to tie two red ribbons on the inside doorknob and keep the door closed all the time.

Recently, I was surprised to run into the same woman again as a principal involved in a bank that wanted a feng shui assessment of a prospective location.

"I'm so glad to meet you again," she greeted me warmly, "as I have been meaning to contact and thank you. I'm the one who followed your advice and within a month, met my future husband. We now have a daughter 18 months old."

COMPUTER

One of the most powerful tools of human civilization and millennium, the computer deserves an important place in our homes and workplaces. Because it is one of communication and creativity, do put yours in N, the water element which governs these two areas in feng shui, W, another area of creativity and because it is created by the element of metal, and SE if you use your computer to generate income, e.g. as a writer, artist, financial, etc.

COPIER

Do put your copier in the SE area of your workplace because it represents multiplication and duplication, symbolically generating abundance, and that's exactly what you want lots of in your business! You can also tie three Chinese coins together with red thread or wrap three silver dollars together in red paper and tape either package to underside of the copy machine.

CRYSTALS

Crystals are very useful in feng shui for placement in an earth element location, as a cure for a variety of ills, as well as breaking up and dispersing *sha* energy from killing or poison arrows.

Next to geodes, natural and man-made crystals are unbeatable for activating love, romance, and relationships in your life, whether you're attracting new friends or commitment to your life, or are keeping your current home fires burning brightly or your partner faithful to you.

These natural stones, especially amethysts, are also valuable for activating knowledge, intuition, metaphysical and spiritual growth, and wisdom. Have you ever noticed that many humanitarians, psychics, and sages are Aquarians whose birthstone is the purple amethyst and who are further empowered by wearing this stone?

Choose your crystals carefully and wisely. You will find the right stones for you at the right time, for you will be drawn to those that are meant for your use. Take each "candidate" one at a time in your left palm, giving each time to respond to your personal energy. As you hold each stone, you may experience a throbbing or tingling, the crystal becoming warm or hot or it may evoke special feelings. You may hear sounds of bells, waves, wind, or music. It may bring about a mood change, or visions of people, places, or things. Pay particular attention to your senses, feelings, and emotions, and physical reactions as you hold the crystals, one by one.

☆ While recently choosing a ametrine crystal in a little store in Otaki, New Zealand, I stood two of them on the glass counter, with their points upward. As I turned away, the larger of the stones suddenly fell over with a large bang, as if to say, "Look at me! " I picked it up first and took it to the West-facing store window where the sun was streaming in. Held firmly in my left hand, the stone didn't react with my energy at all.

Then I went back to the counter and replaced it with the other crystal, which was half the size of the first, a slender and flat stone in shape, and held it so that the point matched the tip of my fingers. As I closed my fingers over it, I could feel an increasing vibration and heat. Instinctively, I knew that my energy had synergized with that particular crystal and it was right for me

If you dream about a certain crystal that you may have dismissed or overlooked, go back and add it to your collection for you were meant to own it.

Remember that it is your energy that adds to the power of your crystal and becomes more and more yours the longer you use and own it. However sometimes, crystals do change and their effectiveness is lost.

Do
❖ Clear your new crystals by running them under cold water (preferably sea, holy, or purified, not tap) to wash away the energies of all the people who have handled them before you. Let the water drip down from the point.

❖ Keep your colored crystals away from sunlight as it will cause them to fade.

❖ You can also clear and purify natural crystals before using them by: gently rinsing them in the ocean if you are fortunate to have access to it, in a sea salt and cold water solution (mixed in a glass or ceramic, not metal or plastic container) , burying them in the earth for at least three days and up to one moon cycle, in rainwater, or stored under pyramids.

❖ Charge up your crystals by placing them out in the moonlight as often as you can.

❖ Put crystals in multiples of two in SW to stimulate love, romance, marriage, and relationships.

❖ Hang two white, red, gold or pink heart-shaped crystals in the SW corner of your bedroom to activate love, marriage and relationships.

❖ Also put crystals in multiples of eight in NE, the area of knowledge, self development, and wisdom.

❖ If you want to excel in your studies or increase your intuitive and thinking powers, put crystals in the NE area of your office, study, or child's bedroom to help her or him do well academically.

❖ Hang a crystal from an exposed beam or from one door frame if you have three doors in a row in a hallway.

❖ Hang a crystal in a dark corner to activate *chi* there.

❖ Put a crystal jar or vase on a desk to deflect the *sha* chi if it is right in the line with a door or corridor.

❖ Dangle a crystal from a window if the view includes corners of buildings, rooftops, lamp posts, chimneys, or an unpleasant view.

❖ Position a crystal over your telephone, fax machine, and/or copier to keep business humming in your workplace.

❖ Clear your birth gemstones after each use or wearing to keep their energies clean.

❖ Use crystals in the earth areas of SW (marriage, relationships, romance, love), NE (knowledge, wisdom, self development) and especially the metal area of W, because earth creates metal which is made into coins, e.g. money.

❖ Place six crystal balls in the NW, (6 being the number associated with this compass direction), another metal area, for bringing supportive people into your life and for strengthening the power and influence of the male head of household.

❖ Find citrine crystals to tuck inside your wallet, as this stone is associated with wealth and fortune. (I am lucky to have citrine and my birthstone for February, amethyst, combined in the beautiful ametrine.)

❖ Consult any of many excellent sources on the meaning of the various gemstones and crystals and healing powers of each.

DESK

If you want to be successful, it is imperative that you place your desk properly. The cardinal rule regarding where to put your desk is that you should always face the door if you can, because symbolically, your business enters from there. Secondly, face one of your four best directions when you are doing most of your work.

Do
❖ Use a desk that has the auspicious dimensions of 35" (89cm) wide X 60" (152 cm) long X 33" (84 cm) high in the material that matches your group: wood and glass for East; metal or stone for West.

❖ If you conducting business from home, it will symbolically come to you through the door, so don't turn your back to it.

Do

❖ Put your desk in one of the following positions, always being aware of where it is in relation to the entrance into the room:

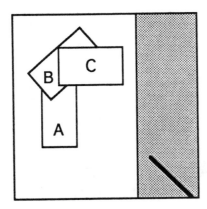
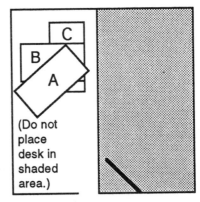

❖ Desks should be facing the entrance to a room, but you should not sit in line with it as you will be in the path of negative energy *sha*.

❖ Your back should be toward a corner or a wall for support.

❖ Place the *bagua* on your desk to help you properly place your accessories, matching the colors and elements. (My easy-to-use **Feng Shui Desk for Success Kit** is designed exactly for this purpose.)

❖ Aquariums and table top fountains are appropriate in E, N, or SE.

❖ Place your personal items on your desk accordingly, taking care that the materials of which they are made matches or creates the appropriate element according to the Generative Cycle, not the Destructive.

❖ If there is disharmony and friction among your coworkers, add more green plants, in multiples of three, for harmony and peace.

❖ Beware of the sharp corners of bookshelves, tables, equipment, storage units, corners of posts, etc. directed toward you or any part of your body.

❖ Have a good balance of *yin* and *yang* when decorating your workspace. Balance light with dark, soft and hard surfaces, smooth and rough textures in the window treatments, furniture, and flooring.

❖ Avoid having any mirrors in your office.

❖ Examine the view you have while sitting at your desk. You should not be directly facing a "killing" or "poison" arrow. Any of the following are considered such: head-on road, curve of a highway or freeway directed toward you, lamppost, fire hydrant, space created by the walls of two buildings, a steeple or pointed roof line of another building, the trunk of a tree, power lines and transformers, edges of signs and billboards, and the corner of a neighboring building.

❖ Try to have more space in front of your desk than behind it.

❖ Put a small fountain or aquarium with black or blue fish in the N of your office or desk as it will activate your business success and career.

❖ Guppies or a single arrowana is ideal for an aquarium constructed of glass (water element) and metal.

❖ Place a geode or round crystal paperweight at the Southwest corner of you desk to enhance harmony between yourself and your coworkers.

Do

❖ Activate the Northwest area of your desk and office so that you will have mentors and support at work. It is a metal sign so you can put anything made of metal or earth (which creates metal) here.

❖ From the chair at your workspace, you should not look out straight into a corridor, or see stairs, storage rooms, closets, elevators, escalators, or toilets.

❖ Ideally, you should sit in the corner farthest from the entrance to the room so as to have a "command" position.

❖ Try to have your back to a wall or a corner which acts as support, but not if there is a corner or post protruding from it. This can be corrected by covering the protrusion with a hanging plant's draping foliage.

❖ Choose the power position in the room whether or not you are sharing it with another occupant. This is the location diagonally across from the entrance and farthest from it. Here you will be protected, sheltered, and will prosper, especially if you have a wall behind you.

❖ Buy or use a new desk or used one whose previous owner expanded and prospered.

❖ Keep your old desk (and office) even after your business has flourished or out-grown its original quarters, as this precious, sentimental piece of furniture contains the energy of your good fortune, much like the goose that lays the golden egg. The same goes for the original office or building in which you made your first million. Many Chinese tycoons keep their modest, even shabby and congested original offices in use as branch locations, long after they have moved into larger, more luxurious or elegant quarters. Others keep remodeling and expanding the original office space in the same building, eventually taking over entire floors or owning the building itself! They never abandon the office space in which they prospered.

☆ Juana and Gus started a mortgage business in the extra bedroom of their home, catering to the Spanish-speaking residents in their neighborhood. Two weeks after my consultation and on the very day that Gus implemented the last, but most critical of the feng shui suggestions that I had made, their business increased spectacularly, from $3000 a month to $35,000! As they planned to move their thriving business out of their home and into a leased site, I advised them to keep a telephone and desk in that auspicious spare bedroom in which they had prospered.

❖ Renovate as much as you wish, but under no circumstances, should you demolish your "lucky" building for to do so is to destroy your prosperity luck and good fortune. Such an action indicates a blatant disregard and disrespect for the uniquely auspicious feng shui of the structure -a very unwise and un-lucky move indeed.

❖ If there are several desks in a room, it is best if they are lined up, e.g., classroom style, all facing the entrance, rather than each other.

❖ If you are the supervisor, your desk should face those of your employees.

❖ Place any of the following on your desk to attract good luck and prosperity: the wish-fulfilling cow, deer, dragon tortoise, *chi ling*, dragon, money tree, prosperity plant, tabletop fountain, crystal paperweight or candy jar.

❖ If your back is to a window, be sure to have a tall building behind you to provide the support of a "mountain."

❖ If your back faces a wall, hang a close up photograph, illustration, or painting of a mountain to give support to you and your business.

Don't

❧ Position your (or anyone else's) desk directly in line with the door or under a beam. You will be in the line of receiving *sha* or under oppressive *sha,* which causes illness, turnover, accidents, other mishaps and misfortune.

❧ Buy or use any desks (or other furniture) previously owned by someone who has gone out of business, bankrupt, been jailed, divorced, etc., no matter what kind of discount or great deal you think you're getting. In the long run, these items will bring ill luck and fortune and negative energy to you, negating any money you saved on their purchase.

ELEMENTS

One of the three key concepts of feng shui and traditional Chinese medicine (TCM) is the elements, their generative and destructive relationships, and the compass directions which they govern. Each element is linked to various aspects of our lives, and putting the right element in the right direction is the proactive way to activate, enhance, or stimulate those areas we wish to improve.

A basic rule of thumb is to place the correct element in its corresponding compass direction, and/or also add the generating element preceding it to reinforce your feng shui efforts. On the other hand, avoiding the destructive relationships which would undermine your feng shui is vital to your work.

Do

❖ Place candles, pyramids, obelisks, and other pointed items in the **FIRE** element of S (fame, fortune, longevity, joy, festivity, protection from evil and bad luck) in multiples of nine. Use the colors of red, blue, and purple in this direction. Enhance your efforts in this compass direction by adding wood which feeds fire. **Avoid** adding the water color of black or water which puts out fire.

❖ Place natural and man-made crystals, geodes, boulders, stones, pebbles, and items made of terra cotta, clay, porcelain, and china in the **EARTH** areas of SW (romance, love, marriage, relationships, motherhood, spouse) in multiples of two, and in NE (knowledge, wisdom, scholarly success, self-development) in multiples of eight. These should be in the earth colors of yellow, white, pink, and red. For example, if you are using wind chimes in these two areas, be sure that they are made of earth materials and not of wood which destroys earth. You can strengthen the earth element by adding the element of fire. **Don't** use any green, tan or wood in SW or NE as it destroys earth by drawing its nutrients from there. Moreover, a tiny seed's root is strong enough to move earth.

❖ Put coins, mirrors, wind chimes, vases, sculptures, and other items made of **METAL** in the areas of W (children, fame, creativity) and NW (fatherhood, helpful or supportive people, benefactors, mentors, international trade, trips, travel) and in N (career business success, communication, creativity) because metal generates water. **Don't** put any fire, red, or pink in metal because fire melts metal.

❖ Locate aquariums, fountains, waterfalls, and ponds in the **WATER** direction of N (career, business success, communica-tion, creativity). As metal is represented by the colors of white, silver, and gold, gives birth to water, it is also compatible with N which is symbolized by the colors black and blue. The metal-and-glass fish tank is the ideal combination for use in N.

Do

❖ Place green plants, flowers, and trees, live or silk, in the **WOOD** area of E (family life, nutrition, health, growth, prosperity, harmony, strength) and SE (wealth, prosperity). To stimulate these aspects of your life, use wind chimes and fountains made from driftwood and bamboo sections instead of metal. Another color that represents wealth is **purple**. Avoid the destructive presence of anything metallic or metal in these two wood areas.

❖ You can also add the color black or water elements such as ponds, waterfalls, fountains and aquariums to these two directions as water nourishes the wood element, e.g., plant life. **Don't** add any white or metal in E or SE as metal, melted and made into shears, scissors, machetes, axes, and saws, destroys wood.

EXERCISE EQUIPMENT

Equipment for improving health, wellness, and your physical fitness are primarily made of metal and belong in the metal areas of W and NW. Because metal destroys wood, **don't** place any exercise machines, such as trampolines, stair, rowing, body-building or weightlifting equipment, etc., in E (health, family life, nutrition, growth, prosperity, harmony, strength) or SE (wealth, prosperity). Nor should any of these gadgets be in your bedroom.

Don't
➳ Don't exercise within two hours of retiring as such physical activity is too stimulating and will delay rest and sleep.

FANS

There are two kinds of fans in feng shui - manual and mechanical. The accordian or flat, hand-held fan is used as a cure for protruding corners or posts to deflect oncoming *sha*, but are hard to hang on 90-degree angles created by two walls converging into a corner. Throughout ancient China, fans were used for ventilation, modesty, creating a cool breeze and for dispersing odors. Fans were prized for their carvings, and later, those that were crafted from fragrant sandalwood originating from Hawaii. In fact, the Chinese name for the Hawaiian Islands was and still is "Sandalwood Mountain." Today paper accordian-style fans are sometimes used as souvenirs of an important occasion with the night's menu written in calligraphy across its folds.

Other than as a feng shui cure on those protruding posts, **don't** use fans as wall decorations, especially in a place of business, no matter how beautiful they are. The word for fan in Chinese is *saan*, a homonym for "to scatter," and represents your business and good fortune being dispersed.

Electrical ceiling fans are popular, common and effective in tropical regions for cooling rooms and buildings. Because they rotate, they resemble screws or bores, drawing energy up and away from a room's occupants.

Do
* For cooling, it is acceptable to install ceiling fans in bed and other rooms, making sure that *they are not located directly* above beds where they will adversely affect the health of the occupants underneath. A ceiling fan can be situated *past* the foot of a bed where it can still effectively cool a room without affecting the people sleeping in it.

* Hand held fans can be carried in your purse, briefcase or satchel and are useful for deflecting the negative energy originating from people. As the tortoise is known for its protective powers, a fan crafted of this animal's shell is especially useful. But a fan of any shape can help deflect *sha*.

FAX MACHINE

The fax machine in your office or workplace represents communication, new orders and ideas, creativity, and developing business.

Do

❖ Keep it clean and in good working order.

❖ Place it in W (creativity), NW (international trade, commerce) or N (communication, creativity.

❖ Tape three coins wrapped in red paper or in a lucky red envelope to the side or bottom of your fax machine to attract auspicious communication from it.

FERTILITY SYMBOLS

If you wish to start or expand your family, you need to put fertility symbols and images to work in several areas: SW (motherhood), NW (fatherhood), W (children), and E (family life). As in all feng shui cures, use the colors, numbers, animal symbols, and elements that correspond to these four directions to activate them.

There are as many fertility symbols as there are cultures. Use whichever you like from yours, or from another, which appeals to your taste, budget, and decorating style.

Do

❖ Put a pair of chopsticks, which literally are called "quick sons/ children" in Chinese, in any of the four directions depending on the material of which they are made: red wood chopsticks in SW; metal or stainless steel ones in NW and W; and wooden, bamboo, or lacquer pairs in E.

❖ Point the chopstick tips away from you and never display them stuck vertically in a bowl of anything, e.g., rice. Standing up like this, the two chopsticks become very unlucky as they resemble sticks of incense placed at the feet of a deceased person at his wake.

❖ Use some other traditional Chinese fertility symbols: picture or painting of the 100 children; a laughing Buddha statue with children climbing all over him; pomegranates; lotus seeds; statue of Kwan Yin, the Goddess of Mercy, representing hearth, fertility, children, and home.

❖ Fill a covered earthen jar with raw rice and put it in SW.

❖ Have fun exploring import shops, native or ethnic arts and stores for fertility symbols to represent the family members: mother (SW), father (NW), children (W), and family life (E.)

☆ When I was pregnant with our fourth child, my husband was shopping at a Chinese supermarket when he stopped in front of a shelf displaying cellophane bags of soup fixings. His eye was caught by packets of lotus seeds among them. Picking one up, he balked at the price for just a few ounces' worth and then put the bag back.

Then he began thinking that we already had two daughters and a son and lotus seeds symbolized sons. What if we didn't even things out with another son, solely due to his stinginess in *not* paying $3.75 for the lotus seeds? The thought too unbearable, he picked up the bag again and added it to his purchases. Yup, it worked. We are the parents of a double girl sandwich!

❖ Put a rocking chair (for nursing or cuddling your infant) with a stuffed white tiger in W or yellow tiger in the SW area of your bedroom and/or home.

❖ The tiger images you put in the W part of your bedroom need not be large or obtrusive, but they need to be of this animal in dignified repose, with or without cubs.

❖ You can also use stuffed or ceramic elephants or pictures of them in SW, matching the material with the compass direction: bronze, gold, copper, pewter, silver or other metal in W or NW; wood in E, SE or S; clay, terra cotta, porcelain, china, or stone in SW or NE; crystal in N.

❖ Paint the SW wall of your bedroom any shade or tint of yellow that you like for earth and motherhood and/or your W and NW walls white for fatherhood.

Don't
☙ Cut any trees or remove any hills or mounds in the NW area of your property as they represent the support of father and protection for your family.

☆ While conducting a training for a San Diego developer, the sales manager told the story of how a homebuying prospect was all set to finalize the purchase on a new home when maintenance workers showed up and cut down a tree on the lot. Promptly, the deal was cancelled.

"The tree was on the NW side of the property," I told him.

He looked at me in amazement and remarked that I must have been psychic.

"No," I laughed, "just knowledgeable in feng shui. By removing the tree, the family's protection was also removed. What they see is what they want and expect. . When an Asian home buyer decides on a house or lot, don't change anything!"

Don't
☙ Decorate with images of fierce, stalking pouncing or attacking tigers with or without live or dead prey.

FILES

The files in your office represent your past, present and future business so do take care of them and treat them with respect.

Do

❖ Keep them off the floor, on higher shelves and bookcases rather than under your desk or table, away from the toilet or washrooms and on the walls on the opposite side of a restroom. This is especially important for your stock certificates, investments, property deeds, and other important documents.

❖ Tape a lucky red envelope with three silver coins or antique Chinese coins strung together with red ribbon on the outside of your ledger books for increased prosperity.

FISH

Who hasn't seen fish swimming around in a pond, tank or an aquarium in a Chinese restaurant? The circulating water represents a flourishing business as well attracts lots of customers. Throughout human civilization, it was the wind and water, e.g., ocean breezes and currents, that propelled ancient sea vessels from island to island, island to mainland, and continent to continent. Communities and cities all over the world that developed beside oceans, rivers, and lakes became centers of commerce and to this day, moving water is symbolic of the prosperity that followed sea trade. So the circulating and pumping of the aquarium water replicates and is symbolic of those same oceans that moved people and goods to wealthy harbors.

The Chinese love things that represent a microcosm of the world and universe - a bizarre rock, bonsai, miniatures, gardens, waterfalls, etc., and fish bowls, ponds, and aquariums with their circulating pumps that simulate the ocean currents.

The very word for fish is *yu* which is a homonym for abundance as well as rain. That's why Chinese don't mind drizzle during the time of the Lunar New Year because lots of rain equates to lots of abundance and/or lots of fish, representing plenty to eat.

The **carp** (*li*) sounds like good fortune (*li*) and the symbols are endless. Fish have always represented prosperity, wealth, and perseverance. It is used in amulets and as talismans against evil, accidents, misfortune and illness. Because of its reproductive abilities, fish represent regeneration, e.g., in families and a pair of fish depicts a joyous sexual union.

Art motives abound with images of fish and water together: men laboring to pull in a full net of fish onto a boat, a child riding the back of a fish or embracing a large carp, etc.

The kind , number, and color of the fish are also significant in feng shui. Fancy koi and common goldfish belong to the carp or *li* family, which is a homonym for prosperity. Keep gold and silver fish as they match the color of coins, e.g., abundant prosperity.

Do
❖ Purchase and release live fish meant for a festival offering or dinner to improve your karma.

❖ Put your aquariums only in living rooms, offices, and studies, <u>not</u> in bathrooms, kitchens, or bedrooms.

❖ Keep fish in multiples of nine in your aquarium or tank, eight of which should be gold in color and one black. If they get sick or die, don't fret but replace them right away for they have absorbed something negative or harmful that was directed at or meant for you.

Do

❖ Maintain your fish tanks, keeping them clean and in good working conditions. Goldfish and koi are cold, fresh water fish that generate ammonia in their watery environment with their waste and uneaten food, which, if not taken care of, can kill them.

❖ Change one third to a half of the water every two weeks to keep this problem under control. Consult your local aquarium shop for assistance in the care and maintenance of your pets.

❖ Keep just one arrowana, also known as the prosperity or "dragon fish." These are beautiful, silvery, gold, or black-tinged ribbon-like fish from South Asia which swim near the surface of the water. They are very lucky and auspicious for your home and business, but are tropical fish and need water heated to about 82 degrees. It grows in proportion to the size of its tank. Although preferring to eat live feeder fish, arrowanas can be trained to eat fish pellets, thus improving your karma in not taking lives.

❖ Place your arrowana in N, W, SE, or NW to activate wealth and prosperity. Learn how to take care of them properly.

❖ Keep an odd number of fish which represents *yang* energy.

Don't

❧ Keep fish or aquariums in bedrooms, kitchens, toilets, or bathrooms, as this is considered unlucky, e.g., loss of fortune.

FLOWERS

Throughout the history of Chinese culture, flowers have commanded reverence and symbolism above all other living plants. The Chinese were expert horticulturists and developed many rare and unique strains of flowers and fruits which we still marvel at and enjoy even today.

Because they generate *yang* energy, flowers and plants should be kept to a minimum in bedrooms, for they are too dynamic and will disturb rest and sleep. On the other hand, flowers are very beneficial for those who are ill, aged, or convalescing, bringing precious, healing *yang* energy to them.

While fresh flowers are best, silk flowers are acceptable as long as they are kept clean and dust-free. Throw out any when they become faded or shabby as this generates negative energy.

Do
❖ Give and use cut flowers to those who are ill to bring them much-needed healing, *yang* energy. Discard them when the blooms wilt or fade and replace them with fresh ones.

❖ Use the colors and symbolism of flowers which correspond to the compass directions and aspects of your life that you are trying to enhance or activate.

❖ Decorate your daughter's bedroom with fresh, photographs, illustrations or paintings of **peonies** which will attract good men to her life and yours if you are *single*. Other flowers that represent relationship-building are **narcissus, plum blossoms, hyacinths**, and **orchids**. Use these in SW, and give them as gifts during the lunar new year.

❖ Images of real or silk peonies in a couple's home should be displayed only in the living room for a harmonious relationship.

Azaleas are popular in Chinese art and represent women, but are highly poisonous so take care not to have them where children and pets may eat or chew on their leaves. They are used in

Chinese medicine for muscle aches and joint pains as well as toothaches, paralysis, and bronchitis. The belief is that small doses of one poison are essential to be counteracted by another.

Chrysanthemums symbolize longevity, dependability, and the wishes for a long duration of anything wonderful: success, marriage, career, etc. Its blossoms are dried for tonics, cosmetics, and sedatives, as well as brewed into a soothing tea for the summer. Paired with plum blossoms, this flower represents an easy life from birth to retirement. Coupled with nine quails, the chrysanthemum symbolizes harmony and peace to nine generations of a family.

The tea is used also as an eye wash. Chrysanthemum ashes are used as a pesticide, and blossoms can be powdered to dispel a hangover. Because this flower comes in such a wide range of colors, do match the color to its corresponding direction.

Jasmine represents women and sweetness and its blossoms are used to scent a popular Chinese tea and are worn in ladies' hair and grown in baskets to provide a pleasant fragrance and deodorizer to rooms. The long blooming plant with delicate pale flowers is ideal for W.

The **lotus** flower is the ultimate symbol of Buddhism, and of purity, joy, and perfection. Because its exquisite blossoms grow from the mud at the bottom of ditches, lakes, and ponds, it represents the potential and possibility that perfection can come from impurity.

Every part of this remarkable plant can be utilized: its leaves impart their special flavor to rice when wrapped and steamed in them; the roots are cut into chunks to create a delicious and nutritious soup, sliced thin to stir-fry with other vegetables or deep fried to create mouthwatering snack chips. The lotus seed, *lien tse*, literally, means "continuous children," is candied or included in a sweet soup for dessert. Combine a single blossom with a bud to represent the ideal partnership; with the magpie, you are relaying wishes for scholarly success to someone; or with a koi in the arms of a young boy, you are sending your wishes for great good fortune and much abundance.

The **magnolia** is the ultimate symbol of a woman who is beautiful, both inside and out, as well as represents a happy marriage. Once upon a time, only the emperor and his family could grow magnolias and its buds, roots, and even the barks are used in traditional Chinese medicine. China has eight species of this beautiful flower, the most distinctive and popular version is white on the inside of its petals and a rose pink or raspberry color on the outside, and is often displayed in wedding motives.

The **narcissus** has the charming name of Water Fairy in Chinese, possesses a delightful fragrance, and is easily grown from bulbs in glass or ceramic containers filled with river stones and water. A traditional symbol of good fortune for the year to follow, the narcissus is forced to bloom right at the time of the Lunar New Year and used for decoration as well as given as gifts to wish someone good luck in business or career. The hyacinth is a lovely companion or substitute to the narcissus. **Do** place these flowers in E or SE (wood.)

There are numerous varieties of **orchids** native to China and these flowers are valued for their extraordinary range of unusual petals and fragrances. Symbolizing the perfect, superior man, love, beauty, refinement, and many offspring. If you desire children, d.o put this flower in SW (yellow, pink, red, or red plants in a clay or terra cotta pot) or W (in a metal container with white or yellow blooms.

Do
❖ Red flowers in the ground or planters on both sides of a South-facing home's front entrance provide protection to your family.

❖ Plant flowers on both sides of a straight footpath if it runs directly from your front door out to the street curb. This strategy will soften the straight line of *sha* energy by slowing it down.

❖ If there is a tree emanating *sha* directly in line with your front door, plant or place two tall flowering shrubs on each side of it to create a triangle pointed away from your home, thus neutralizing the effect of the killing arrow.

❖ Match the color of the flowers to the compass direction your front door faces.

Don't

🙿 Have pictures or vases of peonies in your bedroom if you are already married, for in that room, these flowers encourage your partner to stray or seek love interests outside your home. Peonies belong in living rooms of married couples.

🙿 Keep the pictures of peonies in your home after the single women marry and leave.🙿 Decorate your home with dried flowers, branches, grasses or potpourri, especially in your bedroom. These are all dead and generate *yin* energy, which can adversely affect your sex or love life!

🙿 Accessorize with an overabundance of live flowers or plants your bedroom as they create lots of *yang* in what needs to be a *yin* environment to foster good rest. Three small rooted plants located in the E is quite sufficient to produce oxygen, promote health, well being, harmony, and family accord, all in the domain of E.

FOUNTAIN

A fountain, being a conduit of water, should only be located in N (water) E (wood) and SE (wood). It should not be sited to your right as you leave your home or office entrance. To have a fountain located thus is very unlucky as it encourages unfaithfulness in your relationship.

Do
❖ Choose fountains with water that bubbles or sprays *up* to represent blossoming. The fountain head, e.g., tortoise or fish, should shoot the water *up and/or out* rather than down.

❖ Match the element of the spout or fountainhead to its element, keeping the relationships of the elements in mind. Compatible combinations are water + metal for N, water + wood, e.g., the spout is a bamboo pipe, for E and SE.

❖ Note that the most popular combination of water + earth, e.g., stone, terra cotta, and other earth materials, is really not a correct combination from a pure feng shui standpoint, but acceptable if you cannot find anything else suitable.

Don't
᠄ Use an animal head of any kind as a fountain spout for it is un-natural, representing the creature "spitting."

FRUIT

Fruit symbolize good health and abundance and much more. Altars in homes and businesses always include offerings of fruit to the Kitchen God, Kwan Kung guardian or other deities. These are stacked carefully on small saucers along with flowers, candles, and incense.

A is for **apple** which represents feminine beauty as well as peace as the word for this fruit *ping* sounds like that for harmony.

Apricots with their abundance of Vitamin A are great for beautiful skin and its kernels are edible substitutes for almonds, their ideal ovoid shape is admired in women's eyes or faces.

Do

❖ Keep a bowl or an arrangement of fruits on your dining room table to represent continuous sustenance to your family. Add a mirror on the W or NW wall of your dining room to double the food on your table.

☆ My client moved his large, rectangular mirror from his E wall (wood) to the metal area of W in his dining room and within a week, he received a promotion.

❖ Give potted **kumquat , tangerine** or **orange** plants laden with fruit which are traditional gifts to new businesses or to friends and families during the Lunar New Year as they symbolize giving gold, e.g., prosperity, wealth and abundance for the months that follow.

Pears, symbol of purity and justice, are used to dispel fever, cholera, and dysentery, and its wood is used in making blocks for art prints and wood cutting for books. **Persimmons** commonly come in two types: the plump, round, firm kind which resembles a tomato, and its lantern-shaped relative which becomes soft and juicy upon ripening. This fruit symbolizes joy and festivity and can be placed in S.

Plums are valued for their beautiful blossoms and tasty fruit, symbolizing the season of winter and long life, because the blossoms don't appear until the tree is a ripe old age. The flowers on their branches are often depicted in Chinese art, most notably on the blue and white china, which represents the fragile blossoms floating on water and broken ice at the onset of spring. **Pomegranates** with their abundance of seeds symbolizes prosperity as well as many virtuous offspring who will bring fame and glory to a family.

GARDENS

Let a compass be your guide when designing and planting your garden according to feng shui. You can also use my hands-on **Feng Shui Garden Design Kit** with its built-in compass and stand-up flip book or consult **Designing Your Garden with Feng Shui**. Most importantly, plan and match the materials, shapes, colors, numbers, animals, symbols, purpose, and elements to each of the compass directions to create harmony and balance in your outdoor environment.

When planning your feng shui garden, keep in mind the three major concepts of this Chinese environmental art of placement: the natural flow of the wind and water and beneficial energy, *chi*, *yin* and *yang*, and the compatibility of the five elements with each other. From a feng shui perspective, an English garden has much better feng shui than a formal Italian garden with its straight lines and corners, and precise forms.

Do
❖ Remember that your garden represents a microcosm of the world.

❖ The balance of *yin* and *yang*, light and dark, soft and hard, is achieved through the various materials and plants utilized.

❖ Incorporate curving paths bringing beneficial energy and drawing visitors further into your garden.

❖ Plan a new view, surprise, or delight to be revealed at every step or turn.

❖ Use colors that are subtle, soothing, and harmonious.

❖ Endeavor to create a garden that is designed and executed to look and feel as natural as possible.

❖ Place colors, animals, numbers and elements (C,A,N and E) in their corresponding compass directions.

❖ Your garden should have private and public, meditative as well as active areas - the *yin* and the *yang*.

❖ Features symbolize the harmony and balance between earth, nature, and humans.

❖ The natural flora and fauna are treasured, disturbed as little as possible, and used to their fullest potential.

❖ Remember the most basic law of gardening and life: you reap what you sow. Plant and nurture good seeds of kindness, honesty, compassion, and integrity and that's what you will harvest.

❖ Share your blessings and abundance from your garden, whether it be fruits, flowers, herbs, or vegetables.

❖ If your property is flat, it is considered too *yin*. Create mounds or hills, and add trees, bushes, walls, or hedges to balance with *yang* energy.

❖ Remember to consult the 3 Afflictions chart before you start any major excavating, digging, demolition or construction on your property, e.g., landscaping, installing a pool, etc. or in your yard or garden.

❖ Harmonize with complementary colors, a variety of heights and textures and functions in your holistic garden.

❖ Refer to the following compass guidelines for planning and planting guide for each section of your feng shui garden:

A. NORTH

Color: Black, blue *Element:* Water *Number:* 1 *Season:* Winter *Animal:* Tortoise *Creates:* Wood **Enhanced by***:* Metal *Represents:* Business, career, creativity, personal growth, new ideas, inspiration, prospects, career, music, art, intuition **Destroyed by***:* Earth *Symbol/Shape:* Wave, curve *Use:* Metal, glass, gold, mirrored surfaces, fountains, waterfalls, ponds *Avoid:* Stone, boulders, clay, brick, tile, ceramics, marble, geodes, anything from the earth *Good for:* Metal tool shed, iron fences, antique metal,decorative faucets, metal chimes/mobiles

B. NORTHEAST

Color: Turquoise, tan *Element:* Earth *Number*: *8 Season:* Winter turning to spring *Creates*: Metal *Enhanced by*: Fire *Represents:* Knowledge, self growth, wisdom, meditation, inner journeys, spiritual and intellectual growth, nature, research, experimentation *Destroyed by*: Wood *Symbol/Shape:* Square, rectangle *Use:* Stone, boulders, clay, brick, tile, ceramics, terra cotta, marble, geodes, anything from the earth in multiples of 8 *Avoid:* Wood furniture/accessories *Good for:* Stone benches, steps, block or stone walls, arches, terra cotta wall decorations/sundials/bird-feeders, meditation, reading areas, rock garden, repairing equipment

C. EAST

Color: Green, black, blue **Element***: Wood* **Number***: 3* **Season:** *Spring* **Animal:** *Dragon* **Creates:** *Fire* **Enhanced by:** Water **Represents:** Family, health, peace, sleep, new life and growth, rebirth and rejuvenation, harmony, health, family life, nutrition, healing *Destroyed by:* Metal *Symbol/Shape:* Cylinder, column *Use:* Fountains, waterfalls, ponds, wood furniture/steps/railings, decks, trellises, arbors, bridges *Avoid:* Metal, glass, gold, mirrored surfaces, metal tool shed and gardening equipment/tools *Good for:* Tree houses, secret hideaways, wood swings, vegetable/herb gardens, medicinal plants, fruit trees, morning tai chi/exercises

D. SOUTHEAST

Color: Green, purple *Element:* Wood *Number:* 4 *Season:* Spring turning to summer *Creates:* Fire *Enhanced by:* Water *Represents:* Wealth, prosperity, wealth, abundance, material possessions, communication, perseverance *Destroyed by:* Metal *Symbol/Shape:* Cylinder, column *Use:* Fountains, waterfalls, ponds, wood furniture/steps/railings, decks, trellises, arbors, bridges *Avoid:* Metal, glass, gold, mirrored surfaces, metal tool shed and gardening equipment/tools *Good for:* Prize specimens of anything you cultivate or grow for income, e.g., plants, flowers, fish, vegetables, fruits or even jams, jellies, etc.

E. SOUTH

Color: Red, blue, purple *Element:* Fire *Number:* 9 *Season:* Summer *Animal:* Bird/Phoenix *Creates:* Earth *Enhanced by:* Wood *Represents:* Fame, fortune, festivity, opportunity, dreams, aspirations, awards, fame, achievement happiness, longevity, festivity, reputation *Destroyed by:* Water *Symbol/Shape:* Triangle, pyramids, obelisks *Use:* Outdoor lights, statues of animals/pets, pointed shapes, wood furniture and accessories, pointed trees, pagodas *Avoid:* All water elements: fountains, waterfalls, ponds *Good for:* Burning your leaves, fire pit, barbecue, paladin, wood arbors, trellises, lattices, fences, gate

F. SOUTHWEST

Color: Yellow, pink, red *Element:* Earth *Number:* 2 *Season:* Summer turning to autumn *Creates:* Metal *Enhanced by:* Fire *Represents:* Marriage, relationships marriage. Romance, motherhood, love, relationships, partners *Destroyed by:* *Wood* *Symbol/Shape:* Square, rectangle *Use:* Outdoor lights, pointed shapes, low/flat buildings, stone, boulders, clay, brick, tile, ceramics, marble, geodes, anything from the earth in multiples of 2 *Avoid:* Wood furniture/accessories/fences/arbors *Good for:* Seating/dining for two, e.g., hammocks, romantic motives/ symbols, team sports area, e.g., volleyball, badminton, etc.

G. WEST

Color: White, metallic *Element:* Metal *Number:* 7 *Season:* Autumn *Animal:* Tiger *Creates:* Water *Enhanced by:* Earth *Represents:* Children, social life, children's fame, creativity, harvest, socializing and entertaining *Destroyed by:* Fire *Symbol/Shape:* Circles, arch, semicircle *Use:* Metal, glass, gold, mirrored surfaces, stones, boulders, terra cotta, brick, tile, clay, wrought iron, wind chimes *Avoid:* All fire: barbecues, fire pits, tiki lights, candles *Good for:* Compost, children's garden/play- ground with metal equipment (cushioned in sand), outdoor entertaining, convalescing/healing, bar, sunbathing

H. NORTHWEST

Color: White, gray, metallic *Element:* Metal *Number:* 6 *Season:* Autumn turning to winter *Creates:* Water *Enhanced by:* Earth *Represents:* Travel, helpful people, trade, interests outside of home, international travel, fatherhood, mentors and benefactors, helpful people, supporters, friends *Destroyed by:* Fire *Symbol/Shape:* Circles, arches, arch *Use:* Metal, glass, gold, mirrored surfaces, stones, boulders terra cotta, brick, tile, clay, wrought iron, wind chimes *Avoid:* All fire: barbecues, fire pits, tiki lights, candles *Good for:* Stone/metal statues of deities, e.g., Buddha, Virgin Mary, cherubs, angels, etc., tool shed to store metal tools and equipment, sounds of birds/chimes/water, metal outdoor furniture

GATES

Gates in a garden or to your property should match the color, element, and function of the direction in which they are located.

Good feng shui dictates that the gate be solid if possible and its center should be higher than its sides. When the design is reversed with the sides of the gate lower in height than its center, dipping down, it is considered unlucky for your business and career, even portending failure.

Consult the following list for the appropriate gate for each area of your garden. Although a garden gate is not your main entrance to your home, guests and energy do enter through it. Take care that it is not in the line of any killing or poison arrows.

Do
❖ Use an iron gate with an open design in S to allow beneficial energy to move freely through it. Triangles and pyramid designs are great to incorporate into the gate which could be wood or metal, but do not have any spikes or points at the top of the gate as they will create *sha* energy.

❖ A gate in the SW should be only about half height, e.g., waist or chest, with designs that match the earth element: squares.

❖ In the W, use full height metal gates to slow down as well as obstruct the extreme *yang* energy of the afternoon sun. Use circular, semicircles, and arch designs in this direction.

❖ Arches, semicircles and circles in metal painted blue or black are also ideal design elements for your NW gate.

❖ Take your inspiration from water and the sea as you plan and execute your N gate, embellishing with waves and curves.

❖ As the square represents the earth, this is the best shape for garden gates in the NE.

❖ In the E where the element that reigns is wood, rectangles, cylinders, columns, and poles inspire the design of your gate in this direction.

❖ Your SE gate is also a wood element so do avoid any metal in this area. Use wood planks or boards instead.

❖ Place a full-height, metal gate in W to slow down the overpowering *chi* emanating from the powerful setting sun.

GEODES

Like crystals, geodes are most appropriately in the earth areas of SW to enhance romance, relationships and love, and NE to reinforce your self education and personal development.

HEARTS

Where is love? Whether you left your heart in a certain California city or looking for it in all the wrong places, SW is really where you need to stop in the name of you-know-what and be concentrating your efforts! Heart-shaped candles, and accessories crafted in earth materials such as stone, tile, terra cotta, and clay, and motives with hearts, are best placed in the SW to activate the love, romance, relationships and marriage. Use the corresponding colors of yellow, pink, red, and white.

Do

❖ Hang a crystal chandelier in the SW area of your home, especially if it is where your living room is.

❖ Create a romance corner in the SW corner of your bedroom pictures, paintings, figurines or photographs of happy couples such as Mom and Dad on their most recent big wedding anniversary, in framed with hearts and flowers, doves lovebirds.

❖ Add a gold, red or pink crystal heart in this special place.

❖ Collect heart-shaped containers of terra cotta, china or porcelain or stones from the beach shaped like hearts and in multiples of 2, put them in your relationship corner.

HOUSE

The proper placement and layout of a house is critical to the health, happiness, well being, and prosperity of your family. Choose your lot and home carefully with good feng shui principles in mind. Remember that if it is a choice of what you like and what "calls" to you, almost invariably, the latter will be the better home for you. We also seem intuitively to choose the right house for ourselves at the right time in our lives.

If you pick a house, apartment, condo or other dwelling and everything goes smoothly during the process of your acquirsition, it was meant for you to have it. On the other hand, if there seem to be an inordinate number of delays, obstacles or difficulties during the course of your purchasing and owning the building, perhaps you might reconsider. Heaven always has a greater plan than we and there is a reason and season for everything.

Consult **Appendix A** to determine your best directions that you and your front door should face. Ideally, if you are an East group person, you should choose an N, S, E or SE-facing home. If you are a West group person, select a W, SW, NW or NE-facing home.

The front door should accommodate the main bread-winner of the home, whatever the gender, and the best (*Sheng chi*) or 3rd best (*Tien yi*) directions are best for front entrances to face, although any of the best four directions are acceptable.

Knowing your best feng shui directions empowers you from this day forth and is extremely advantageous to you in life. You can apply this powerful information to every other situation and will begin noticing that the good things that come to you will originate from those four directions.

For example, when asking for a raise or promotion or are negotiating, you should face your best (optimum) area. Feeling under the weather today? Try facing your 2nd best (health) direction as much as possible to receive the beneficial healing energy all day. If you wish to improve or further a relationship with someone, on your date or during a discussion, face your 3rd best direction which represents harmony at work, home and in relationships. And anytime when you feel at a disadvantage, insecure or vulnerable, be sure to look toward your 4th best or best direction for protection.

❖ Consider your property as a whole and plan accordingly. If possible, the house should be at the center of your property.

❖ The best lots and house shapes are square or rectangular, which represents balance and completeness.

❖ Your house should be level with the road or situated above the grade so that you walk or drive up, not down, to it. The incline to the building should not be long and steep, representing difficulty.

❖ The ideal feng shui location is a site with a hill behind, two smaller hills in the near front, facing a wider, farther view, preferably of water.

Traditionally, the front of the house should face S, but any direction that has the classic horseshoe/armchair configuration is advantageous. If your home's front entrance faces one of your best directions, it becomes even more auspicious for your and your family.

❖ Mountains are too *yang*, especially if they are very close to your property or are pointed, young mountains (rather than rolling hills which are very old). Create some distance between them and your house, or choose another lot.

❖ Your home should not be at the junction of intersections that resemble a Y, T or L. (see below), or at the outside of a curved street. Just use automobile headlights as your guide. If any shine onto your house, either fully or partially, that area of your building is affected by *sha* energy, the killing arrow.

These can all be mitigated by the installation of the concave mirror which will protect your house and its occupants by absorbing the *sha* and not send any of it back out to harm anyone else, e.g. drivers.

Do
❖ Be aware of poison arrows directed toward your home. These can be in the form of the following:

- Lamp posts
- Gables
- Pitched roofs
- Steeples
- Signs
- Fire hydrants
- Roads
- Bridges
- Tunnels
- Corners of buildings
- Temples, shrines, schools, government buildings, churches, hospitals
- Rivers, streams and lakes
- Telephone and electrical poles and transformers
- Power lines and towers
- Trees

❖ Houses that have negative space in their footprints have "missing corners." These can be metaphysically restored by adding something that matches the *element* of that area after its compass direction is determined.

For example, if the missing area is in W or NW, a metal pole, e.g. flag pole, can be installed. If the negative apace happens to be in SW or NE, both earth areas, add two large boulders or a grouping of 8 stones to that area, and so forth.

Stand outside your house at approximately where you think the "missing corner" is, facing your house. Stretch one arm directly toward one exterior wall, and then extend your other arm toward the second wall. Move until you are standing on the exact spot where the two walls would converge if they had been extended, using your outstretched arms to help you envision the walls. Mark the apex on the ground for the proper replacement of that absent corner. (See illustration on the next page.)

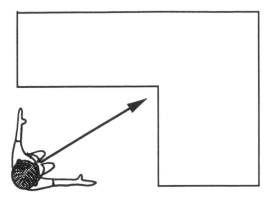

Do

❖ Move the holy and sacred statues of deities into the house
first. Next, bring in the rice, salt, oil, money tree, and master bed
into your new home. Gather your family and while holding
hands in a circle of faith and love, say a blessing or have a holy
person bless your home before you move in.

❖ Be aware of poison arrows inside your house too. These may be
in the form of:

  ⮞ Long hallways
  ⮞ Corners
  ⮞ Stairs
  ⮞ Doorways
  ⮞ Doors
  ⮞ Beams
  ⮞ Columns and posts with corners
  ⮞ Protrusions from the wall, e.g. light boxes on ceilings or
    corners of covered posts

❖ Also keep in mind the three major concepts of feng shui: how the
energy flows, the balance of yin and yang, and the generative and
destructive cycles of the elements.

❖ Your house position should also have good feng shui, especially
if it is situated on a hill. An ideal spot is about halfway up the

slope, not at the bottom so that the hill or mountain hovers over your dwelling, nor at the very top where it may lack protection from the elements, as the building would be too exposed.

The top four houses below are in good locations, the others are not for they are below grade, top of a hill, under a cliff, at the end of a cul de sac, too close to a hill or on the outside curved of a road.

❖ You *can* have a house that faces a hill, if the house has flat land in front of it and the hill is not too close. Mountains emanate tremendous *yang* energy so you need to put some distance between them and your home. There really is a comfort level in that distance and you need good intuition (Does the mountain *loom* over your house?) to sense how close or far away the hill can be before it feels oppressive and menacing to you.

❖ Consult the ba-gua and its corresponding directions and C, A, N and E religiously to aid you in furniture placement and accessorizing your home for harmony and balance.

INGOTS

Chinese gold ingots are shaped like deep hulls of boats and are the equivalent to Fort Knox's gold bars. These can be piled onto the decks of model ships displayed facing *into* the room in your home or office, or in groups of three in the metal element areas of W or NW.

KITCHEN

Your kitchen is the place in your home from which your family's wealth and prosperity originates. Keep its lights and appliances, the burners on your stove in particular, clean, free of clutter, and in good working order.

You should not see your kitchen as you enter the main entrance of your home, for to do so, you will be preoccupied with food and may find yourself battling weight problems.

Do

❖ Keep your elements of fire and water separated. The stove (fire) should not be located directly across from the sink (water), e.g., on a peninsula or island, or too close to the sink on the same counter laterally.

❖ While model homes usually show a number of decorative items on the counters, in reality, good feng shui dictates as little as possible in sight on kitchen surfaces to facilitate good *chi* flow.

❖ Put your most often-used utensils in the corresponding areas to their elements, e.g., water in N, wood in E and SE, metal in W and NW, etc., taking great care to avoid putting them in their destructive cycle positions. For example, to put your knife holder in E would be to sever family harmony and health. In this case, it's best to store knives out of sight, in the W.

❖ Use colors and light to create balance and harmony in your kitchen.

❖ At mealtimes, whether your family dines in your kitchen/nook or dining room, ensure family harmony by having each member sit *in* his/her corresponding direction: father in NW, mother in SW, eldest son in E, eldest daughter in SE, youngest son in NE, middle daughter in S, middle son in N, youngest daughter in W. Chinese dinner tables are round or octagonal to accommodate these arrangements.

Don't
➢ Locate your aquarium or table top fountain in your kitchen. Because it is the domain of the elements of fire nourished by wood, the element of water will destroy your prosperity.

KNIVES/SWORDS

No matter how many movies or images you have seen of ceremonial cutlery being presented or exchanged as gifts, in general, knives and swords do not make good gifts to anyone as they emanate *sha* energy and represent the severing of relationships.

Any items which have been used to take lives carry especially bad karma and bring bad luck to those who own or keep them. It is best that they are stored away, with their points down, wrapped up or kept inside their scabbards. If they simply must be displayed, here are a few guidelines.

Do
❖ Hang the knife/sword on a wall securely so that its point is facing a corner.

❖ Display your weapons on a counter or wall racks especially designed and made for this purpose, taking care that their points are not aimed toward any person entering or occupying the room. Better yet, store them inside a locked cabinet with doors.

❖ If giving a pair of scissors or set of knives or swords as a gift, attach a penny to each blade to neutralize the severance effect. The pennies are to be returned to the giver.

Don't

☛ Mount a pair of crossed swords over a doorway or path as that will shorten the lives or adversely affect the health of those who pass through that entrance.

LIGHT/LIGHTS

Light is one of the most important components of feng shui as it symbolizes *yang* energy. Light, airy rooms with good circulation are one of the best ways to improve feng shui in your home or workplace. By increasing the amount of light in any environment, you have taken an immediate, easy important step to improve feng shui there.

Do

❖ Keep all rooms bright without glare by opening up shades and curtains or using window treatments with light-filtering properties.

❖ Keep trees in your yard and garden trimmed and properly pruned so as to allow sunlight balance out the shade and shadows.

❖ Balance the dark and light colors and textures in all of your environments, starting with darker shades on the ground and lightening up walls all the way up to the ceilings.

❖ Add more wattage to lighting fixtures to improve the *chi* in dark corners and corridors.

❖ If there is a negative space or "missing corner" to your L-shaped house, preventing it to becoming a square or rectangle, add a light aimed toward the inside corner of the yard.(see A below)

❖ If your house is situated below the grade or street level (see B below), add a light pole that is directed toward the top of the house.

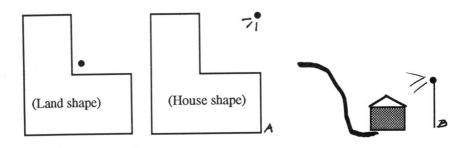

(Land shape)   (House shape)   A   B

❖ Bring light into your home by installing a mirror (on a W or NW wall only) to reflect a pleasant outdoor view.
❖ Use a flat or round mirror to reflect back obtrusive street or signage lights shining at your house or through your window.

LITERATURE

The Chinese have also revered learning, and literature and classics have been an integral part of the culture, memorized and quoted by young and old alike throughout the course of Chinese civilization. The most learned men surrounded the country's emperors who valued them as much if not more than his military advisors.

Son without learning, you have raised an ass.
Daughter without learning, you have raised a pig.
-Chinese proverb

Paper was one of China's most enduring gifts to the world, and the printing on it with wood and stone blocks created the first books, paper currency and playing cards. Although the *movable* printing press revolutionized bookmaking, printing on paper was a major contribution to the world. It is no wonder then, that books and literature as well as those poets, philosophers, and writers from which they originated, were considered treasures of the country.

The spoken word, not as enduring as faded ink.
-Chinese proverb

Among the great classical literature of China is the *I Ching*, the Book of Changes. It is believed that every imaginable change that takes place in the universe falls into one of the 64 possible forms. The *I Ching* is used today both superficially for fortune telling as well as for the deeper philosophical contemplation of the meaning of and exploration of life, nature, and the universe.
Generally speaking, only a few books should be kept in your bedroom. Too many books become too stimulating and should be kept in your study, office, living room, or library.

Inspirational literature, biographies about successful people, personal growth, and self-help books should be placed in the N (business success, career) area of your home or room. **Reference** and **motivational** books, cards, and posters in the NE (wisdom).

Literature about **starting/developing new ventures/life/ business/beginnings** belong in the E (growth; spring) and those about **wealth building, increasing your investments and assets**, in the SE (wealth, material growth, fortune).

Gifts, books, pictures, and other items about and from celebrities and fame have their home in S (fame, fortune), and literature **about international relations, trade, travel, leadership, organization, organizing, planning, and your business card files** belong in the NW.

LIVING ROOM

Next to the kitchen, living rooms can be the heart of the home or they could be rarely-used showplaces in houses that boast a family or great room.

If not often used, they are a great place to place your altar(if this room is in your fourth best direction), statues of Good Luck, Good Fortune, and Long Life, books, arrangements of peonies to keep your happily-married state activated. On the floor, under furniture, figurines of the three-legged toad of wealth can be tucked out of sight, and this room is most ideal for enjoying music, art, or literature, and for entertaining your family, friends and other guests.

Your living room is one of the most perfect locations for your aquarium with the single arrowana or dragon" "prosperity fish, koi, or a community fish tank with an odd number of fish.

MIRRORS

Mirrors are mostly used in the BSTB School of feng shui to reflect as well as introduce light into an environment, deepening a flat or closed space, deflect negative *sha* energy, replace "missing corners," opening up confined areas, and generally act as an all-around panacea for bad feng shui.

They are considered one of its 9 Basic Cures, the others being: lights, wind chimes and bells, plants and flowers, fish bowls and aquariums, moving objects, heavy objects, electrically-powered object, and bamboo flutes.   When positioning a mirror, be sure to put it where it does not cut off any part of your reflected head, for to do so is very unlucky indeed!

Do choose the appropriate mirror to do the job, being mindful that in feng shui we strive to improve our own lives without harming others.   Remember that karma is always in action and to practice your feng shui for yourself or others with a pure heart and strong intent.

Ba-gua mirrors come in many forms, but what makes them so powerful (and dangerous) is that they always have the eight trigrams of the *I Ching* positioned around the round mirror.   Use these powerful cures with great caution.

These are the "big guns" that you use to face bad neighbors by reflecting back their negative energy, giving them a dose of their own medicine (see details under **BAGUA**).

Any flat, eight-sided mirrors is also called *bagua* which can be found at craft and art supply shops where they are sold for reflecting figurines for tabletop display. In feng shui, these are the most harmless of cures to reflect back the trunk of a tree or a lamp post, for example, that is facing your home's main entrance.

They are also very good to use facing a street is directed toward your home or business that may have a school or another inhabited building at the end of it and you are taking care not to send back any harmful sha.

Concave mirrors with red plastic rims and shaped like the <u>inside</u> of a bowl are used to absorb negative energy without sending anything back out toward its source. These mirrors also turn the images they capture upside down like a fun mirror at a carnival.

In a pinch if you can't get to a Chinatown to purchase one of these, you may substitute a small, shallow stainless steel, silver, or pewter cereal, candy, or mixing bowl. Position it so that the inside of the bowl faces the offending street, dumpster, building, or other origin of *sha*.

Ba-gua mirrors are only to be used outdoors and installed above the doorframe. The only exception to this is if you live in a high-rise building on an upper floor, for example, across from one of the angled corners of Hong Kong's Bank of China building or directly facing one of the killing arrows emanating from San Francisco's TransAmerica pyramid-shaped headquarters. Then you can safely put your bagua mirror in a sliding window track, right up against the glass, with the mirror and trigrams FACING OUT and the mirror back facing into the room.

☆ Having advised several of my clients to use a bagua mirror with its trigrams to deflect the negativity from their undesirable next-door neighbors, I was told that they were very effective, causing the neighbors to move away.

Convex mirrors are those that protrude or bump out and these are the most dangerous of all when they are surrounded by the trigrams of the I Ching. These are the ultimate weapon, you might say, reflecting back whatever image and energy it receives, such as very bad sha directed at you. **Do** exercise prudence and great caution when using these for your action may backfire against you, causing mishaps and misfortune.

Flat mirrors are the least powerful, but do their work quietly and unobtrusively. A mirror of any size or shape can act as deflection of sha energy when directed toward its origin. A small compact with a mirror or a hand mirror is a handy protective tool for carrying with you. If you encounter negative people or happen to be positioned in line with a poison arrow, such a common item is very useful for reflecting back the offending image or object without calling attention to it.

I have advised substitutes for mirrors with positive results: metal door knockers which have shiny or polished surfaces, silver platters or trays and even pewter plates.

✩ Pat's neighbor across the cul de sac was a disagreeable fellow whose house was angled so that a corner pointed directly at her front door. Since installing a ba-gua mirror outside her home or entrance would be obtrusive as well as mar the beauty of the exterior, I came up with a creative solution for her to ward off her neighbor's negative energy. A polished silver tray on a stand was positioned on a sideboard right across from her front door, acting as a deflecting mirror. A month later Pat called with thanks and appreciation from herself and her neighbors. The unpleasant man had moved to another city.

✩ At one of the top Lexus dealerships in California, a new showroom was in the process of being completed when I was called in to conduct a feng shui consultation. Some of the staff who were familiar with feng shui had expressed concern that the new facility had inauspicious features.

Sure enough, the building's front entrance directly faced toward two massive, cylindrical posts that supported a huge promotional, electronic billboard located next to the freeway, a stone's throw away.

Hanging a traditional, tri-color ba-gua mirror on above the self-opening glass doors to deflect these two sources of *sha* would have been both obtrusive and incompatible to the architecture of the building. The solution I recommended was to install highly reflective metallic window coatings on the doors and the windows flanking them.

LIBRARY

A library in a home or office suite reflects the refinement and education of its owner, its collection of books and literature indicative of self-development and personal growth. NE is the appropriate area for locating a library for fostering wisdom and knowledge. It is a good place to study, read for recreation or growth, house a piano or other musical instruments.

The shelves on which books are stored can emanate negative energy directed to those who occupy the room, so take care to move the books' spines flush with the edges of the shelves.

MONEY

If money makes the world go around, then we all need to be prosperous to keep the earth spinning on its axis! At the beginning of human civilization, shells, stones, bones, metal, gems, animals, women, beads, jewelry, sacks of grain and many other things served mankind as currency. But it was not until the Chinese printed on paper with wooden blocks and ink that paper currency was invented in 1005 AD. Can you imagine how liberating it was to carry this "pocket money?" No longer would people have to lug around money made from all those other heavier materials!

If you want to activate your money-increasing abilities, look to the N (business success, career), S (fortune, prosperity), E (fortune), and SE (material wealth, prosperity). Remember to use the corresponding colors, numbers, animal symbols and elements to stimulate your wealth.

Do
- ❖ Give lucky red money envelopes generously and freely as gifts for they are traditional and appropriate for every happy event. This includes birthdays, anniversaries, weddings, opening a new business, housewarming, engagements, lunar new year and other festivals, graduations, seeing a new baby for the first time or family members after an absence - just about any joyous occasion. The custom is that you put paper currency or a check

inside and they are great for tucking into a greeting card. Aaah the best melding of Eastern and Western social practices! It is also traditional for the payment to the "wind-water doctor" to be enclosed in a red packet or paper.

Even after a Chinese funeral, those who have attended are handed two small packets when they leave. One contains a coin wrapped in white paper, symbolizing mourning and *yin*; another in red paper for *yang* and good luck.

The one rule concerning these red envelopes is that while everybody, both wed and unwed, can receive them, only <u>married</u> folks can give them to other people. Married people, you see, are considered lucky for they represent being complete and a pair, e.g., two halves of a whole, the *yin* and *yang*, dragon and phoenix.

❖ "Plant" a metal box filled with coins of a high denomination the W or NW area of your property. Remember the generative cycle of the elements? The earth gives birth to metal and this symbolism is very strong as metal, literally "gold," in Chinese, likewise originates from the earth. It is particularly auspicious if you happen to already have a hill or mound of earth in either of those directions on your property. But remember to consult the 3 Afflictions chart for the year before you bury your treasure.

If not, **do** create your own symbolic mountain by making a mound from earth at least three feet high and burying the cash box under it. If the mound is in the NW, even better, because this is the compass direction that represents the head of the household, as in father, so that outstanding feng shui will be created, affecting the whole family. (Also see **CASH BOX/REGISTER** and **SAFE**)

Your **checks** for deposit at the end of the day or week should be kept in the W part of your business, office or desk until you are ready to go to the bank. West represents autumn and harvest time and reaping the fruits of your labors.

Safes, most of which are constructed of metal, should be placed in either W or NW (both of the metal element) in your home, office or business. Just like the mound of earth in those directions represents the father, the safe symbolizes the prosperity and financial security of a family.

NUMBERS

To the Chinese, numbers have great symbolism and meaning, mainly because they are homonyms for other, lucky words. Telephone numbers and area codes, bank accounts, street addresses for homes and businesses, final purchase prices on homes, automobile licenses - all of these and everything that is affected by numbers and digits in Chinese or Arabic, are taken into consideration and analyzed for their sounds and symbolism.

It is important to note that the Chinese language consists of nine major dialects and thousands of regional and local ones. What sounds and means something in one of these dialects may be neutral or negative when spoken in another. In general, the Southern Chinese who speak the Cantonese dialect have more meanings associated with their numbers.

A prime example, for instance, is the Los Angeles offices of the Chinese Daily News in Monterey Park, California, with the street address of 1588 Corporate Center Drive. When spoken in Cantonese, "One, five, eight, eight" sound exactly like saying, "Guaranteed, no, prosperity, prosperity." No self-respecting Cantonese would move into, much less, build or work in an "unlucky" structure in which he would be unlikely to prosper. On the other hand, while saying these same four numbers in the Mandarin dialect may sound like any number of the other 250,000-plus words in the Chinese language, the combination has no unlucky denotation or connotation at all.

Numbers are also associated with the eight compass directions, the magic Lo Shu square, and numerology. In feng shui placement, you can put that number of items or enhancements in its corresponding area, along with its color, animal or other symbols, and elements. For example, the number of E is 3. You can put three (number) wooden (element) dragons (animal symbol) in that direction to activate family life, health, nurtrition, harmony, prosperit, etc. In S, whose number is 9, you can put nine (number) red (color) candles (fire) in that part of your room, study, or home.

The Southern Chinese were the first to hear about other countries across the oceans because Whampao, ten miles down the river from Canton (leave your weapons and women behind, thank you) was the only city where the foreign ships were permitted to dock. Immigrants who had been farmers and shipbuilders for generations were the first to arrive in what was to become the United States.

In 1788, ninety smiths and carpenters were on board two ships, the *Felice* and the *Ephigenia*, arriving in the fall at the west coast of Maui, Hawaii. Already, over 100 years before, Chinese had immigrated to British Columbia where they were building ships without written plans or speaking any English.

The earliest Chinese immigrants to every part of the globe were from the coastal cities of the south and spoke the Toishan subdialect of Cantonese. With them, feng shui, the lunar calendar and annual festivals, their thousands of years of science, technology, and discovery (paper money, playing cards, stirrup, compass, gunpowder, wheelbarrow, metal plow, irrigation, mechanical and agricultural knowledge, etc.) and Confucianism traveled.

It was these pioneers who first exported feng shui around the globe, following its *yin* practices when burying their dead who could not return to the homeland, and *yang* forms for the living when laying out their communities all over the world. From Singapore and Australia, from London to Brazil, wherever you find Chinese communities, the traditions of feng shui are sure to follow.

The following is a list of the homonyms for the numbers in the Cantonese dialect:

1: <u>Sounds like</u>: guaranteed, ensure, honor
<u>Represents</u>: North, practicality, rich, comfortable and balanced lifestyle, success in business and career, prosperity luck, water, tortoise

2: <u>Sounds like</u>: Easy, double
<u>Represents</u>: Southwest, love, romance, relationships, mother-hood, the mind and intellect, earth

3: <u>Sounds like</u>: Life, birth, growth
<u>Represents</u>: East, trinity of heaven-earth-man, mind-body-spirit, spiritual number, emotional strength or weakness, prosperity, harmony, health, nutrition, wood, dragon

4: <u>Sounds like</u>: Death, to die/kill
<u>Represents</u>: Southeast, wealth, material goods, abundance, rational intelligence, logic, high discipline, wood

5: <u>Sounds like</u>: Not, no, nothing
<u>Represents</u>: Center, human feelings, spiritual number, earth

6: <u>Sounds like:</u> Longevity, wealth, deer
<u>Represents</u>: Northwest, father, helpful and supportive people, mentors and benefactors, international trade, trips, travel, metal

7: <u>Sounds like</u>: Guaranteed, ensure
<u>Represents</u>: West, children, creativity, children's fame, soul-searching, metal, tiger, auspicious number from present until 2/4/04 when the current period of Chinese time ends and 8 replaces it

8: <u>Sounds like</u>: Prosperity, growth, expansion, multiply
<u>Represents</u>: Northeast, knowledge, intelligence, scholarly success, wisdom, self-development, experience, education, fertility, auspicious number beginning on 2/5/04 (beginning of the Period 8 in Chinese time) the more 8s you have in your life, e.g., phone, house number, social security, bank account, etc., the more prosperous you will be for the next 20 years, when 9 (for Period 9) replaces 8 in 2024.

9: <u>Sounds like</u>: Long life, dragon
<u>Represents</u>: South, fame, fortune, joy, festivity, longevity, recognition, awards, celebrity, fire, phoenix or bird.

0: <u>Represents</u>: Infinity, forever, eternity

Now you can easily see how combinations of these numbers can be considered lucky or unlucky. For example, 28928 (my house number) equates to "easy prosperity, long life, easy prosperity." 541-8818, my phone number, says " not to die, guaranteed double prosperity, guaranteed prosperity." 528, the model number that German auto maker BMW could not market or sell successfully in Hong Kong and Singapore, told prospective buyers that they would have "no easy prosperity." And 1400, an office, building or home street address stands for "guaranteed death forever and ever."

(You can find a wealth of information regarding other sales and marketing strategies and cultural pitfalls in my book **TARGET: The U.S. Asian Market,** *A Practical Guide to Doing Business*.)

OFFICE

Because our office in or away from home is where we create our prosperity, its importance in terms of feng shui.cannot be minimized.

If you love your job, you will never work a day in your life.
- *Confucius*

Keep in mind that feng shui is all about harmony and balance. Your existence is unbalanced if you spend too much time at work, neglecting your family, health, mind, and spirit.

Remember that this ancient art of placement is only one of the four legs of an imaginary table. To practice it while neglecting the other three – physical, emotional, and spiritual, is to dilute feng shui's effectiveness.

Don't be one of those who are so busy making a living that you forget to live. There are no guarantees in life we learn painfully as we journey through it. Live each moment as if it were the only moment you have to live.

Yesterday is a memory, tomorrow is a mystery, we only have today, and that's why it's called the present.
-Anonymous

When deciding on a place to locate your business, follow these general guidelines:

Do
❖ Choose an area of the country or your city whose *element* or compass *direction* matches the nature of your business. You can refer to the following chart.

East (Wood, rebirth, growth, health, new beginnings)
Artist/Design studios
Catering
Child care
Children's centers
Health careers
Hotels
Hospitals
Medical careers
Plant nurseries
Restaurant

Southeast (Wood, health, prosperity)
Medical facilities
Trade

South (Fire, fame, fortune)
Athletics
Entertainment
Media

Southwest (Earth, relationships, marriage)
Agriculture
Building
Churches
Civil engineering
Construction
Drilling
Mining
Pottery/Firing/Kilns

West (Metal, commerce, finance, children)
Accounting firms
Air Conditioning

West (continued)
Banks
Child care centers
Computer hardware
Jewelry
Loan
Financial planning
Manufacturing
Mortgage companies
Parks/Playgrounds
Recreation
Refrigeration
Savings
Securities
Stock brokerage
Workshops

Northwest (Metal, trade, travel, helping people)
Import/export
Travel agency
International business of any kind
Human resources
Personnel
Psychology
Psychiatry
Therapy and counseling

North (Water, commerce, business, cleaning, communication)
Advertising and Public Relations
Art
Brewing
Cleaning
Communications
Computer software/hardware
Creative writing

North (continued)
Distilling
Dry cleaners
Exchange
Janitorial service
Laundromat
Literature
Media
Music
Oil
Word Processing
Writing

Northeast (Earth, knowledge, wisdom)
Colleges
Information technology
Libraries
Trade schools
Universities

❖ Choose a building that is in proportion to its neighbors.
   Those on either side should neither dwarf your building,
   nor should yours tower over theirs.

❖ The architecture of your building should be compatible
   with that of your neighbors.

❖ The building should not face a cemetery, exterminator,
   mortuary, pawn shop, school, government office,
   hospital, funeral home/parlor, etc.

❖ An office should not have a skylight.

❖ The area behind your or anyone else's desk should not be a
   traffic zone.

❖ Avoid putting bizarre or strange objects on your desk.

❖ Keep the cords to your office equipment well hidden.

❖ Take care that a corner of another building is not directed at the main entrance of yours, nor at you and your desk through a window. Install a mirror (see **MIRRORS**) to mitigate the *sha* energy of that killing arrow.

❖ Associate with positive, successful people. Avoid negative colleagues and coworkers who generate *sha* with their complaints, grumbling, and finding fault, which drags down morale and effectiveness in a workplace.

❖ Bring live flowers and plants into your workplace if it has a lot of electronic or technical equipment to create more balance with soft curves and colors.

❖ Utilize low-maintenance house plants such as the prosperity bamboo (see details under **PLANTS**) which flourishes in just water and light, either artificial or natural, and ideal for business or home work environments.

❖ Be sure to discard wilted or dead plants and flowers as they are a source of *sha*.

❖ Avoid exposed beams situated above your chair or desk.

❖ No doors should be located behind you.

❖ Your desk should not share the wall with a toilet nor should you face a toilet door or someone else's sharp desk corner.

❖ Pay attention to the physical conditions at your workplace:
    -Lighting, both natural and artificial
    -Odors

-Temperature
-Air conditioning
-Heating
-Distractions from traffic in halls
-Water cooler
-Employee snack/lunch areas
-Food odors
-Perfumes and scents
-Proximity to fax and copy machines
-Proximity to other employees
-Volume of conversation around you
-Loudness of telephones

❖ People create their own energy too. Evaluate your company's culture which is just as important as the environmental atmosphere.
❖ Is it supportive to all employees?
❖ Does the environment facilitate personal and professional growth?
❖ Are there cliques among the employees?
❖ Is diversity considered a strength or hindrance?
❖ Is the culture inclusive of employees in or exclusive, creating envy, hostility, friction or dissension?
❖ Is there a strong sense of teamwork that creates synergy, or is it every man or woman for himself or herself?
❖ Does everyone share the company and management's vision, mission, and passion?
❖ Are there opportunities for advancement?
❖ Is the person in charge a leader or a boss?
❖ Does he or she lead by example, value each person's strengths, abilities and talents by putting them to best use for the growth of the employee and company?
❖ Is the leadership style one of example and encouragement, or one of fear and intimidation?
❖ Does the company have clear goals and objectives which are regularly reviewed, discussed, and revised by all?
❖ Are the contributions of every employee recognized?

Remember that your work environment should be conducive to harmony, teamwork and synergy and contribute to your productivity and prosperity. If you are the person in charge, strive to be a great and inspiring leader.

PICTURES

From scratchings on cave walls to photography to digital animation, humans have created as well as recorded images of themselves and their world since they evolved. Some of these pictographs developed into written languages such as the Egyptian hieroglyphics and Chinese characters which are still in use today through thousands of years of its history.

Introduce art you love into your environment, being mindful of feng shui principles. In feng shui, images from nature is preferable to abstract art which may have too many sharp points and angles, which in themselves create poison arrows. Impressionist art such as that of Renoir, Van Gogh, Matisse, etc. is ideal for homes and offices with their pleasant subjects and soft but vibrant colors.

When applying the elements to artwork, remember their two relationships: generative and destructive, and put the proper artwork in the corresponding direction. Some combinations are not compatible, for example. If you are trying to activate business success and career of N, don't put up a picture of earth and water, e.g. a scene of water coming through rocks or gorge or canyon, because earth destroys water. In this case, if you simply *must* have the art, water should dominate among just a few, insignificant rocks.

Do
❖ Put water and wood, such as a forest with a river running through it in E and SE (water nourishes wood).

❖ Put water-only pictures, such as surf/waves/sea and scenes/
waterfalls/streams/lakes in N (water). If there are elements such
as wood (trees, etc.) or earth (mountains, rocks, etc.), be sure
that the water portion dominates.

❖ Place earth images such as mountains such as the Matterhorn,
Mt. Fuji, McKinley or Whitney, the Sahara, Himalayas, the
Alps, Andes, Grand Tetons, Grand Canyon, Half Dome at
Yosemite, Guilin's distinctively-shaped mountains, Mt. Rush-
more, the Great Smoky Mountains or the Rockies, etc. in SW or
NE (earth).

❖ Your fantastic pictures and photographs of Hawaii's, South
America's or Italy's volcanoes erupting , campfires, or fire-
places and other fiery subjects belong in the S (fire).

❖ Hang photographs of metal sculptures and subjects that
you admire such as Calder's mobiles, Golden or Brooklyn
Bridge, Eiffel Tower, etc. in W or NW (metal). Yes, you
can have pictures of ships, but no, it's better if the Titanic,
and other ill-fated or shipwrecked vessels are not among
them!

❖ Check out the balance of *yin* and *yang* in your artwork.
If you are female, are most of your paintings filled with
female images? If you are male, does most of your art
reflect traditionally male interests such as hunting, fishing, sports
and automobiles? Remove and replace some of it with artwork
that includes the female gender, especially if you are interested
in stimulating love and romance or want to find a partner in
marriage.

❖ Activate your love, romance, relationship and marriage
area of SW in your bed or living room by putting up pictures
that have happy couples in them, e.g. Mom and Dad on their
25th+ anniversary, a photograph of your brother and his bride on

their wedding day, a poster depicting sweethearts and couples holding hands, kissing or embracing. Frames should be of porcelain, terra cotta or china.

❖ Hang a picture of a mountain or a forest behind for support in your office, and face a picture of water or a field of flowers facing you as you sit at your desk, again, keeping in mind the elements and their relationships.

❖ Put images of food and fruit in the E of your dining room to represent abundance and sustenance always on your table and in your home.

❖ Animal and bird images should match their directions. (see **ANIMALS** and **BIRDS**)

Don't
❧ Hang pictures of war, etc., battlefields, cemeteries, etc. , e.g., Picasso's Guernica or Dante's Inferno, death, e.g skulls, or gloomy scenes, people or sad faces.

❧ Pictures of pouncing or attacking animals, fierce birds, and any dead fauna are to be avoided in your home or office, if they are depicted as maimed, dismembered, bleeding, decapitated, or killed by violent or brutal means.

❧ Put water scenes above your head in your bedroom - they suggest your being smothered or drowned.

❧ Hang too many pictures of birds and other feathered creatures in your dining room.

❧ Put paintings or pictures of water behind your desk, nor should you place a picture or photograph of water, e.g., a river, flowing directly toward you.

PLANTS

All plants give something to the world and to us. How impoverished we would all be without the countless species of plants in the world.

Next to the lotus, bamboo is probably the most valued and revered of all Chinese plants. There are thousands of species of **bamboo** native to China and just as many uses for this valuable and versatile plant which has been always one of the most enduring images associated with its native land. Rice is packed into its leaves and folded into an ingenious wrapper and cooked to lend its unique flavor -the original fast food! The bamboo plant's shoots are diced, sliced and added as a staple to many dishes. Its cane is fashioned into every imaginable utensil and tool from toothpicks to chopsticks, scoops to spoons, water pipes to rattan and wicker furniture and accessories, to the incredible and fantastic scaffolding upon which construction workers stand to erect Asia's high rise buildings.

Like the **oak** in Western culture, the bamboo symbolizes strength, endurance, constancy and above all, long life, but this amazing plant is often used as a metaphor for being strong as well as flexible, rather than unbending. A mighty wind might blow down the oak which resists, but the same wind can pass right through bamboo leaves and the plant's cane, although heavy and thick, can flex and therefore withstand the wind's power.

For long life, plant lots of **pine** trees in the southern part of your property. These plants are symbolic of longevity because they live many years and because they contribute to good health by producing much oxygen. Standing in a pine forest or grove to do your exercises is believed to be the most healthful location for you.

Another plant that represents long life is the **juniper**, but do not use the Hollywood juniper on your property for it resembles claw-like fingers.

Prosperity bamboo looks and acts like a delicate version of a dracaena plant. It flourishes in just plain water and either natural or artificial light, and has the ability to sprout new shoots when cut just above a cane section, thereby "multiplying." Sections can be put into water and grow new roots. So maintenance-free and yet slender and elegant, this plant's stems can be trained by bending into tortuous shapes which are greatly admired.

The prosperity bamboo is best in E or SE to stimulate the aspects associated with those areas: family, health, harmony, nutrition, prosperity and abundance. They make lovely gifts to give to friends, relations and new business startups, when put in a clear glass or crystal vase tied with a big, red ribbon.

The **jade plant** is distinguished by its rounded leaves which are plump with water, to enable this succulent to retain its moisture for long periods of time. Another easy to grow bush, a stem with leaves can be broken off from the mother plant, placed into soil and on its own, takes root, making it very simple to propogate. It makes a welcome addition to any interior or exterior of a home or business as it symbolizes good fortune and wealth. They are ideal for placing in the wood areas of E and S.

Man-made jade plants are simulated by threading and twisting gold wire into semi-precious stone "leaves" onto an artificial, potted bonsai tree and bestowed as a gift which relays wishes for prosperity and abundance. These stone trees are perfect for placement in the earth areas of NE and SW.

There are several live versions of the "**money tree**" : jade plant, plumeria, ginko, poplar, prosperity bamboo, among them, any of which can be planted in the SE or E section of your yard to activate your wealth. Then there are the man-made money trees which are silk trees upon which fan-folded, crisp and brand-new currency is hung with red thread. Sometimes these artii\ficial trees are festooned with miniature gold ingots or lucky red money envelopes stuffed with high-domination currency. Do give these unique creations as gifts for any special occasion, especially weddings, birthdays, graduations, and grand openings of any enterprise.

The **willow tree**, although graceful and lovely to look at, is associated with sadness and should not be planted on one's pro-perty, nor should you plan to hold your marriage ceremony under one.

Don't

↝ Give a bonsai plant as a gift to anyone as it symbolizes limited growth and therefore is unlucky.

↝ Use any plants in your home that have sharp, spiky leaves or which have thorns, barbs or needles on them, such as **cacti**, all of which are the source of tiny poison arrows directed at the occupants of a room.

Such plants should not be planted in the close proximity to the front entrance to or flank the path leading up to your home. On the other hand, these "hostile" plants when installed on the perimeter of your property some distance away from your home create a natural deterrent to intruders.

REFRIGERATOR

Although this major appliance stores and preserves our food which provides us with nutrition (normally associated with E), it is manufactured out of metal and therefore should not be placed in the wood areas of E or SE where it would destroy the wood element.

RICE

This marvelous grain is one of the essential staples to much of the world's population. It represents survival, prosperity, sustenance, fertility and abundance. The Filipinos give a sack of rice as a housewarming gift to bestow blessings of abundance.

Your family's rice storage container should be covered to protect it from critters and bugs. Whether made of plastic or porcelain, it should be stored away from sight and to ensure continued prosperity and abundance for your family, tuck three antique or silver coins in a lucky red envelope at the bottom of the rice. Change the packet before the Chinese new year annually.

A pinch of raw rice mixed with sea salt is tossed into every corner of your home after smudging (cleansing) to purify it, and rice in a covered porcelain urn is ideal as a fertility symbol to place in SW for motherhood.

SCULPTURES/STATUES

Artwork in the form of sculptures and statues as well as figurines should be placed according to the element and life aspect that matches the corresponding directions. Metal in W and NW, earth materials in SW and NE, wood in E, SE (or S to feed the fire element.)

Do
❖ Harmonize the subject matter of sculptures and statues also with its direction or the aspiration you desire. For example, you might use "The Thinker" in NE to stimulate knowledge and self-cultivation.

❖ Place earth or metal versions of Rodin's "The Kiss" or a pair of Mandarin ducks, swans or doves placed in SW to attract a partner in your life.

❖ Put carved wooden dragons in E for health, strength, vitality, family life, and harmony.

❖ Position a pair of sculpted metal cranes at the center of a water element in the N area of your garden or business to foster business success and career.

STAIRS

Stairs are conduits of energy, channeling it up or down, in or out of your rooms, different floors, house and workplace so it is critical that you pay attention to where they are facing. They also exert pressure on anything under them.

Do
❖ Avoid occupying desks, offices, bedrooms, beds and seating that are facing stairs or under them.

❖ Your stairs should not face a toilet.

❖ Stairs that directly face your front door and/or continue out to the curb represent your family's prosperity pouring down and out of your home.

❖ When assessing the feng shui of a multi-storied home, the direction that the top step of the landing of each floor faces represents the entrance to that floor. Take your compass reading from this point.

Don't
✒ Place an altar, cash box or register, or bed under stairs.

✒ Your front door should not be at the bottom of any stairs, as in a basement apartment below grade or street level. Negative energy runs and collects in lower spots, just like drainage water.

STUDY/LIBRARY

The very best location for your study or library in your home is in the NE, the area that governs knowledge, wisdom, self-improvement and enlightenment. If you are fortunate to have walls and shelves, arrange your books according to subjects, once again matching them with their corresponding areas.

Do

❖ Encourage your children to study in the library or study if their own room does not have a suitable NE corner.

❖ Use your study or library also for other enriching, cultural activities such as playing music, meditating, reading or practicing a musical instrument.

❖ Donate books that you no longer use, want or need to schools, churches, hospitals, halfway homes, libraries, prisons, or other institutions

❖ Store your books with their spines flush with the edges of bookshelves to eliminate sha energy. Even better is to use cabinets that have doors on them

❖ Put your aquariums or fish tanks in these rooms.

❖ If you are a married couple, you can enjoy your fresh or silk display of peonies in your study or library.

SWIMMING POOL

Generally a swimming pool is considered dead water. If you have no choice and must use plastic or concrete, do your best to hide it under foliage or some natural materials. It's best to have a kidney-shaped, oval or round pool so there are no sharp corners.

The corner of a swimming pool with straight sides creates *sha* energy and should not point directly to the house, especially a bedroom.

TELEPHONE

One of the most useful and important tools of modern-day communication, the telephone represents business coming in to you.

Do
❖ Tape three Chinese coins to the underside of your telephone to encourage it to ring more or you can hang a hollow-rod wind chime or crystal above it.

TOILET

Because they are sources of unpleasant odors, *sha* and are carriers of waste, toilets must be located with care.

Do
❖ Keep the seats, covers and doors to toilets closed at all times, especially if the toilet faces a bedroom or it directly faces the door to the bathroom leading to a hall or another room.

Don't
❧ Have a toilet in the center or SE (wealth) areas of your home.

❧ You shouldn't see a toilet as you enter your home nor should one face the front door.

❧ Your toilet should not be located on a second floor directly above your front door or beyond the front wall of your home. Both of these locations spell major calamity or disaster to your

family.   Use earth colors in that toilet to suppress its negative
energy or place a large stone on top of it to destroy the
flushing away of your family's wealth. Avoid using it.

ے Toilets should not be facing bedrooms, altars, kitchens, dining
rooms, kitchens, or share a wall with any of these rooms.

TREES

Hug and thank a tree because today it gives so much to you
– a feeling of peace and tranquillity, shade from the sun's harsh
glare and rays, oxygen into the air for your good health, something
beautiful to look at, fruits and flowers for you to enjoy, materials
from which so many wonderful things come: paper, furniture,
accessories, art and sculpture, utensils like chopsticks and salad
tongs, bowls, sailboats and ships, and the list goes on and on.

Old trees are considered holy and sacred and possess strong
energy so try not to cut any down. However, if they are diseased or
damaged by lightning, etc., you may have to remove the dead
branches or the entire plant. This is particularly critical if you have
sick or elderly family members living in your home.

The leaves of trees represent the bones of the occupants of
a house and should not touch the building as they will draw away
chi from it.

Do
❖ Plant roses, although they have thorns, have a pleasant scent
which neutralizes the *sha*.

❖ Plant evergreen trees with broad or rounded leaves, rather than
with pointed leaves.

❖ Keep trees healthy for good feng shui, for even bare branches
pointing toward your house can create *sha*.

❖ Two small trees or statues can flank the door and act as guardians to your home.

❖ Trees can create a lot of *yin* energy because of their shade. Keep all trees on your property topped and thinned out to allow the *yang* energy of the sun to penetrate through their branches.

❖ Trees are generally beneficial if planted some distance away and not up next to the house, and not singly so as to dominate your entire back yard or garden.

❖ Trees represent wealth, prosperity, and abundance so keep them healthy and trimmed.

❖ Trees behind a property offer protection, particularly if in the N.

❖ Trees planted in a row or curving around the house, like arms embracing it, symbolize wealth and good luck.

❖ Dense trees behind a home are lucky, but allow some distance between the two.

❖ In your front yard, plant your trees in multiples of threes, sixes or nines.

❖ Tree stumps can be covered with any sort of creeping vines or ivy, or with a large potted plant situated on top of them.

Don't

☙ Plant or have a tree at the center of your house.

☙ The trunk of a tree should not be facing your front door as it will block your view of the world outside and obstruct beneficial *chi*.

☙ Watch the shape of the trees which should not resemble any animals or creatures.

WATER

Without this marvelous resource, there would be no life on our planet, nor feng shui. Representing trade and commerce, water has always been associated with prosperity because it was on sea vessels on water, powered by the breeze that brought goods from faraway lands.

In feng shui, water is one of the most important elements. Ancient water classics detailed how wealth traveled to a home by the way the water flowed toward or away from it. Here are some guidelines to follow:

Do
❖ If the flow of traffic or water in front of your house is curving or slow-moving, it is considered auspicious. If the flow is rushing or is located *behind* your house, it carries away your family's prosperity.

❖ A water element on the LEFT side (looking out) of the door is fine, but balance it with trees on the right.

❖ Water elements are good feng shui additions in your front yard only if it faces N (water element.)

❖ Water, which is *yin*, can be balanced with the *yang* of large boulders protruding from it, or by allowing sun or artificial light to reflect from its surface.

❖ Add more yang around your water with the use of color, sound, colored tiles or river stones, living creatures such as fish, or water plants.

❖ A pond surrounded and darkened by deep woods or dense trees is overwhelmingly *yin*, imbalanced and not good feng shui.

❖ An oyster-shaped pond should be enhanced with a focal point where the "pearl" (a large stone, fountain, gazebo or pavilion) would have been.

❖ Water features, such as a kidney-shaped pool curving around the house, attracts money but the addition of a whirlpool, fountain, spa, or jacuzzi keeps the water moving changes it from *yin* to *yang*.

❖ Water features are best matched with natural materials such as stone, wood and earth.

Don't

➣ Never put a pond or fountain near the right side of the door (looking out), for it will encourage infidelity in your partner. However a tall statue or piece of sculpture matching the *element* of the front entrance is acceptable.

➣ Put any fountains, ponds, or other water elements in front of your main entrance if it is facing South which represents the element of fire, symbolizing fame and fortune. Water destroys fire. If there is *sha* aimed toward your front entrance, a water element can weaken its negative power.

➣ Hang a picture that has predominantly water in it over your bed. This is akin to being underwater, e.g., drowned.

WIND CHIMES/SOCKS

Wind chimes and wind socks uplift our spirits, activate stagnant energy, and suppress negative influences. In general, they should be only used in the compass directions associated with the material of which they are made: bamboo or wood in E, SE and S; metal in W and NW; terra cotta, stones, etc. in SW or NE; and crystal or glass in N.

Do

❖ Use chimes with 6 or 8 hollow rods to activate or draw energy up.

❖ Use chimes with 5 solid rods to suppress, exhaust, or destroy an element or bad luck, e.g., direction of the5 Yellows.

❖ Use in NW to attract good friends, partners, supportive or helping people, mentors and benefactors into your life or 2 or 9 rod chime of crystal or other earth materials in the living room.

❖ Hang a set of small chimes of exposed beams, but not if they are in a bedroom.

Don't

▪ Hang wind chimes in a bedroom, office or indoors except in the living room.

ZODIAC

Do

• Refer to the chart on page 29 and wear and decorate with your personal Chinese zodiac animal symbol for protection.

Appendix A

Personalize your best directions according to your birthday. Consult the Lunar calendar on page 23 to find your birth year's kua number, then refer to the chart below for your 4 B(est) and 4 W(orst).

| KUA | Men | | | | | | | | Women | | | | | | | |
---	Best	2nd B	3rd B	4thB	4th W	3rd W	2nd W	Worst	Best	2ndB	3rd B	4th B	4th W	3rd W	2nd W	Worst
1	SE	E	S	N	W	NE	NW	SW	SE	E	S	N	W	NE	NW	SW
2	NE	W	NW	SW	E	SE	S	N	NE	W	NW	SW	E	SE	S	N
3	S	N	SE	E	SW	NW	NE	W	S	N	SE	E	SW	NW	NE	W
4	N	S	E	SE	NW	SW	W	NE	N	S	E	SE	NW	SW	W	NE
5	NE	W	NW	SW	E	SE	S	N	SW	NW	W	NE	S	N	E	SE
6	W	NE	SW	NW	SE	E	N	S	W	NE	SW	NW	SE	E	N	S
7	NW	SW	NE	W	N	S	SE	E	NW	SW	NE	W	N	S	SE	E
8	SW	NW	W	NE	S	N	E	SE	SW	NW	W	NE	S	N	E	SE
9	E	SE	N	S	NE	W	SW	NW	E	SE	N	S	NE	W	SW	NW

Get an accurate reading of your building's compass direction by facing OUT while standing at your front entrance. Utilize your important rooms, master bedroom, office, dining, family and living areas in your BEST areas and those of lesser importance, such as bathrooms, kitchens, toilets, closets, garage and storage in your worst areas. Match each family member to his/her chart. Check the next Appendix for what Best, 2nd B, etc. mean. For example, Best=growth, vitality and prosperity.

Appendix B

What the Best (and Worst) Directions Mean

Feng shui is the Chinese environmental art of placement that harmonizes our personal energies with that of the earth and the universe. Your birth date, month and year each possesses their own unique energies. In order to receive them, you should FACE, as much as possible, the specific four compass directions based on your horoscope. This strategy will ensure that all aspects of your life will go smoothly as you encompass the blessings and benefits.

Everyone in the world belongs either to the East group (best directions are N, S, E and SE, not necessarily in that order) or West group (best directions are W, SW, NW and NE, not necessarily in that order). Notice that your group's best are the worst for the other group and vice versa.

Best (*Sheng Chi- Breath of Life*) Growth, vitality, prosperity. Most auspicious for your front entrance or your head pointing here during sleep. Face this direction when sitting at your desk, negotiating or anytime on the phone. Do not block or put kitchen or toilets here. 2nd Best (*Tien Yi -Heavenly Doctor*) Face this direction as much as possible if you are ill or have poor health. The plug of your rice cooker should face here. Good for dining room or a bedroom for a convalescent. 3rd Best (*Nien Yi - Long life with wealthy offspring*) Activates harmony and peace at home and work, as well as relationships, love, marriage and romance. Also good for front door to face. 4th Best (*Fu Wei - Good fortune position*) Provides protection from bad luck and evil. Your kitchen stove should be *across* from here. Good location for back door, bedrooms, altars, and for sleeping with your head pointing toward this direction.

Worst (*Chueh Ming - Severed Life*) Total loss, accidents, illness, disease and death. Do not choose a home with its front door facing this direction. Protect yourself and be extra cautious when facing or travelling toward this direction. 2nd Worst (*Liu Sha - Six Killings*) Legal problems, bad health, fatigue, setbacks, frustration, maybe death. Good for storage, kitchen, toilets, and closets. 3rd Worst (*Wu Kwei - Five Ghosts*) Discord, friction, quarrels, fighting, betrayal, fire and burglary. Good for toilets and kitchen. 4th Worst (*Ho Hai - Accidents and danger*) Mishaps, losing court cases and accidents. Don't put your bedroom, office or study here. Good for toilets and storage.

INDEX

The Practical Feng Shui Chart ©
(Compass School Bagua)

© Angi Ma Wong 1992

ANGI MA WONG *Feng Shui Lady*™

Born in China as the daughter of an industrialist and diplomat, Angi Ma Wong grew up in New Zealand, Taiwan, Hong Kong, and Washington, D.C. She is an award-winning businesswoman and consultant to the new Four Seasons Hotel and Tower in San Francisco, Universal Studios, Motorola, Paul Anka Productions, Longo Lexus, Bank of America, COTY Inc., The Limited, Crustacean Restaurant, San Antonio Winery, Dragon Noodle Company, New York Life, California Gift Show and over 100 international commercial and residential real estate developers worldwide.

A recognized authority and popular feng shui lecturer/practitioner/writer, she has presented to international and national conferences and audiences. Among them are the London International Feng Shui Conference, 4th Feng Shui Conference (Orlando), Color Marketing Group, Pacific Coast Builders Conference, Chicago Merchandise Mart, Pacific Design Center, National Assn. of Home Builders, Urban Land Institute, Pacific Asia Museum, etc.

Angi with fellow experts Grand Master Yap Cheng Hai, James Mosher, and Professor Lin Yun at the 4th Feng Shui Conference in Orlando, Florida.

Ms. Wong has appeared on OPRAH, Regis and Kelly, CNN Headline News, Discovery Channel, Learning Channel, CBS Sunday Morning, TIME magazine (7/3/2000), all network television and in over 300 feature articles, including the *New York Times, Wall Street Journal, Los Angeles Times, Chicago Tribune, Seattle Times, Philadelphia Inquirer, Asian Week, San Francisco Examiner, USA Today, Entrepreneur, Bride, Opportunity World*, CNNfn.com, homestore.com, fastcompany.com, Soul-utions, *Craftrends,* SW Airlines *Spirit* and *The Atlantic.*

Her work includes: **Feng Shui Room-by Room Home Design Kit, Feng Shui Dos and Taboos 2003-2005 Page-a-Day © Calendar** (Storey Books), **Feng Shui Dos and Taboos for Love (Hay House), Feng Shui Dos and Taboos for Financial Success** (Hay House) **Feng Shui Desk for Success Tool Kit, Feng Shui Garden Design Kit, Designing Your Garden with Feng Shui, Wind-Water Wheel:** *A Feng Shui Tool for Transforming Your Life,* **The Practical Feng Shui Chart Kit, Woman's 4-Minute Bible, Baby Boomer's 4-Minute Bible, Been There, Done That:** *16 Secrets for Success for Entrepreneurs*, **Practical Feng Shui Chart Kit, Night of the Red Moon** and the award-winner, **TARGET: The U.S. Asian Market.**

❖❖❖

To schedule Angi for a personalized residential or commercial consultation or to speak at your next conference or special event, **call (310) 541-8818 or email amawong@worldnet.att.net**

FENG SHUI LADY ™ line

Quan.

___ Feng Shui Dos & Taboos (alphabetical, new info, 400+ tips, easy, all levels) @$17.95 ea....	$ _____
___ Feng Shui Room-by-Room Home Design Kit(w/clear PFS chart, book,compass)@$24.99ea...	$ _____
___ Feng Shui Desk for Success Tool Kit (w/clear PFS Chart, compass, book) @$24.99 each...	$ _____
___ Feng Shui Garden Design Kit (moisture-proof w/compass, book) @$24.99.	$ _____
___ Feng Shui Wheel (2-sided, for Compass & Black Sect schools) @$24.99 ea.	$ _____
___ The Wind•Water Wheel (personalized best, worst directions by horoscope)@ $19.95 each.	$ _____
___ Feng Shui: *Arranging Your Home to Change Your Life* @ $14.95 each.	$ _____
___ Feng Shui Dos & Taboos (gift size) (400+tips, one per page)@$8.95 each.	$ _____
___ Simple I Ching (easy to use and do) @ $10.95 each.	$ _____
___ Large concave "Big Bertha" mirror (high voltage power lines, etc.) @ $20 each.	$ _____
___ Large ba-gua mirrors (neighbors, buildings, walls, etc.) @12.00 each.	$ _____
___ Stone turtle(small; put in N for career, business success)) @ $5 each	$ _____
___ Stone turtle (large; for N, E SE for wealth, career)) @ $10 each	$ _____
___ Live prosperity plant 8" (grows in water, care instructions inc.)@$5 each.	$ _____
___ Chinese smudge stick (for cleansing negative energy w/instructions)@ $3 each.	$ _____
___ Crystal heart (love, marriage, relationship) @$20 each.	$ _____
___ 3 legged prosperity toad (Large 4") $20 (Small) $16 each.	$ _____
___ Dragon tortoise (prosperity, protection from 3 Killings) @$35 each	$ _____
___ Chinese coin hanging for prosperity $12 each.	$ _____

Pacific Heritage Books-ORDER FORM B

____ Windchimes (Pagoda w/5 rod hollow) $10.. $_____

____ Double happiness character (love, marriage) @ $5 each................ $_____

____ **Feng Shui Lady** compass ball keychain @ $5 each .... $_____

INSPIRATION & GROWTH

____ California Coastal Adventures:*Beaches, Boat Trips, Islands & Marit.Museums* $14.95 ea... $_____

____ Woman's 4-Minute Bible: *Lifelong Lessons for Personal Empowerment*@$8.95 each.... $_____

____ Baby Boomer's 4-Minute Bible: *Enduring Values to Live By* @ $8.95 each.......... $_____

____ Been There, Done That: *16 Secrets of Success for Entrepreneurs* @ $14.95 each...... $_____

Subtotal $_____

Calif.residents add 8.25% sales tax $_____

ALL orders shipping & handling add 10% of subtotal $_____

Overnight____ Priority Mail____ (Pub. will add correct amt.) $_____

for the TOTAL AMOUNT $_____

Check enclosed ☐ VISA ☐

Money Order ☐ MC ☐

PLEASE PRINT CLEARLY BELOW:

Name _____ *Phone* (_____) _____

Address _____ *City* _____ *Zip* _____

Cardholder name (print) _____ *Signature* _____

Account No. _____ *Exp.ires Mo.* ____ *Yr.* ____

ORDER TODAY! Pacific Heritage Books Box 3967-02OF, Palos Verdes, CA 90274-9547 (OF 1/02)

Call 1-888-810-9891 (310)541-7178fax order View items @: wind-water.com *or* FengShuiLady.com

(International orders must be prepaid by credit card in US dollars and shipping will be charged by weight)

My Personal Feng Shui Notes

My Personal Feng Shui Notes

My Personal Feng Shui Notes